Here's One i Made Earlier

120 fabulous recipes from the popular cookery show

An Action Time Production for Channel Four

Ebury Press
London

1 3 5 7 9 10 8 6 4 2

First published in the United Kingdom in 1997 by Ebury Press
Random House, 20 Vauxhall Bridge Road, London SW1V 2SA

Random House Australia (Pty) Limited
20 Alfred Street, Milsons Point, Sydney
New South Wales 2061, Australia

Random House New Zealand Limited
18 Poland Road, Glenfield
Auckland 10, New Zealand

Random House South Africa (Pty) Limited
Endulini, 5A Jubilee Road, Parktown 2193, South Africa

Random House UK Limited Reg. No. 954009

A CIP catalogue record for this book is available from the British Library

ISBN: 0 09 185443 1

Here's One I Made Earlier
An Action Time Production for Channel Four
Series devised by Executive Producer: Stephen Leahy
Producer: Tony Nicholson
Director: Martin Scott
Associate Producer: Valerie Pye
Set Design: Taff Batley

Designed by Jerry Goldie Graphic Design
Printed and bound in Great Britain by Mackays of Chatham plc, Kent

CONTENTS

FOREWORD

To take three chefs and ask them to create a three-course meal may seem a perfectly reasonable request but when you introduce the complications of recording four programmes in a day and need every dish to be duplicated for the cameras in several different stages of preparation, that's when the fun begins.

The 'Cooks' Club' set is at Granada's Studio 6 in Manchester, which used to be where all the interior scenes of *Coronation Street* were recorded, so we have come a long way from The Rover's Hot Pot to culinary expertise. The three chefs on camera are supported by a big team – our backstage preparation kitchen has a staff of 11! The 'Cooks' Club' members are viewers who have written to us requesting tickets and we presume that they are keen on food as there is always a rush for the tasting tables!

The production team have had great fun recording the 120 episodes to date and we appreciate the many letters and phone calls that the recipes and chefs inspire.

No TV show gets on screen without a huge effort and I would like to thank the eight chefs – Tessa Bramley, Jean Davies, Amanda Grant, Paul Heathcote, Aaron Patterson, Greg Robinson, Steven Saunders, Mark Wogan and our on-screen wine expert Patrick Whenham-Bossy; our Commissioning Editors Fiona Chesterton and Julia Lestage, together with the television crew: Tony Nicholson, Martin Scott, Nicholas Ferguson, David Crean, Valerie Pye, Andy Coates, Shelly Chadwick, Taff Batley, Jane Wilson, Anne Stirk, Dean Simpole-Clarke, Colin Capon, Pat Peacock, Jessica Leech, Dave Eager and the Granada Studio Crew.

Stephen Leahy, Executive Producer
Here's One I Made Earlier
Action Time Ltd
Manchester

Starters

Steven Saunders

Chilled Tomato And Basil Soup

SERVES 4

1 cucumber, peeled and deseeded

2 cloves garlic, chopped

12 ripe tomatoes, peeled and deseeded

1 tsp white wine vinegar

juice of ¹/₂ lime

200ml (7 fl. oz) double cream

salt and pepper

large sprig of fresh basil

fine dice of cucumber and tomatoes

small sprig of fresh mint

Put the cucumber, garlic, tomatoes, vinegar and lime juice into a food processor and blend to a smooth liquid. Add the double cream and blend again. Season to taste. Finely chop the basil and add to the finished soup.

Pile a garnish of cucumber and tomato dice in the centre of the chilled soup bowl and pour the chilled soup around. Garnish with a small sprig of fresh mint.

Paul Heathcote

Broad Bean Soup

SERVES 4

450g (1lb) broad
beans (shelled
weight)

600ml (1 pint)
vegetable stock

1 level tsp sugar

1 level tsp cornflour

1¹/₂ tbsp water

300ml (¹/₂ pint) single
cream

45g (1¹/₂ oz) butter

sea salt and pepper

Simmer beans and stock for 18 minutes with sugar. Purée and pass back into the pan. Moisten the cornflour with the water and the stir in the cream. Stir into the bean purée. Bring back to the boil. Add the butter and blitz with a hand blender.

Paul Heathcote

Roasted Asparagus With Crushed Potatoes And Sour Cream

SERVES 4

450g (1lb) asparagus

3 large baking
potatoes

125g (4 oz) butter

salt and pepper

150ml (¹/₄ pint)
whipping cream

chopped chives

¹/₂ lemon

olive oil

Trim asparagus and boil in salted water until cooked. Refresh in cold water. Boil potatoes in their skin until cooked. Drain and peel. Crush potatoes with the butter with the back of a fork. Season with salt and pepper.

Whip the cream, season with salt and pepper and add the chives and a good squeeze of lemon juice.

In a hot pan, fry the asparagus with the olive oil, season. Place the crushed potatoes in a bowl, rest the asparagus on top and cover with chive cream.

Marinated Tomatoes With Parmesan

SERVES 4

250ml (9 fl. oz) olive oil, to cover goats cheese

4–5 cloves garlic, crushed

450g (1lb) tomatoes, sliced

4 individual goats cheese, crostinis

4 slices brioche bread

450g (1lb) rocket leaves

225g (8 oz) fresh Parmesan, shaved

3 tbsp balsamic vinegar

seasoning

Mix the olive oil with the crushed garlic. Put the sliced tomatoes into this flavoured oil and marinate for 1 hour with the goats cheese on top. Turn the cheese in the oil. Place a goats cheese on to each brioche slice and cut with a 7.5-cm (3-inch) cutter over cheese. Bake in the oven at 200°C/400°F/Gas Mark 6, basted with some of the marinade for 10 minutes.

Remove sliced tomatoes from marinade and arrange in a circle on the plate. Put some rocket leaves in centre and garnish with curls of Parmesan around. Remove goats cheese from the oven and put in the centre of tomatoes on top of the rocket leaves. Blend the balsamic vinegar with the marinade, season to taste and dress around the cheese. Serve.

Jean Davies

Aubergine And Cheese With Tangy Tomato Sauce

SERVES 4

1kg (2¹/₄ lb) large aubergines, halved

2 tsp olive oil

1 clove garlic, crushed

6 tsp plain flour

100g (3¹/₂ oz) fromage frais

3 free-range eggs

60g (2¹/₂ oz) Pecorino cheese, grated

60g (2¹/₂ oz) Provlone Picacante (or other mature hard cheese), grated

salt and freshly ground black pepper, to taste

1 red pepper, peeled and finely chopped

3 tsp basil, finely chopped

Tangy Tomato Sauce

3 tbsp extra virgin olive oil

1¹/₂ tbsp walnut oil

750g (1lb 10 oz) tomatoes, skinned, cooked and cooled

1¹/₂ tbsp raspberry vinegar

Preheat oven to 190°C/ 375°F/Gas Mark 6. Put aubergines cut side down on a baking sheet and place in oven for about 45 minutes or until soft. Leave to cool. Lower temperature to 180°C/350°F/Gas Mark 5. Peel off aubergine skin, mash the flesh and squeeze out moisture. Place the flesh in a blender with olive oil, garlic, flour, fromage frais, eggs and cheeses; blend until smooth. Add salt and pepper to taste.

Butter a ¹/₂ litre (about 1 pint) terrine dish and line with buttered greaseproof paper. Pour in half aubergine mixture and smooth. Cover with chopped pepper and basil, then the remaining aubergine mixture. Smooth top and cover dish with foil. Place in a large dish or roasting pan containing 2.5cm (1-inch) depth of water and cook in the oven for 55–60 minutes or until the terrine is firm to touch. Allow to cool, then chill for several hours.

To make the sauce, put all the ingredients in a clean bowl, whisk well and season to taste.

Deep Fried Brie With Onion And Cassis Marmalade

SERVES 4

450g (1lb) brie

6 tbsp flour

1 egg, blended with a dash of milk

6 tbsp breadcrumbs

175g (6 oz) baby onions, fresh or frozen

100ml (3¹/₂ fl. oz) red wine

3 tbsp cassis or biackcurrant cordial

1 head radicchio

1 head oak leaf or lollo bianco

3 tbsp olive oil, approximately

seasoning

sprig of chervil

Cut neat 7.5-cm (3-inch) rounds from the brie. Flour, egg and then breadcrumb the rounds twice to ensure the coating will hold the cheese while frying.

Prepare onions by cooking in a 2:1 mixture of red wine and cassis and cook for approximately 15 minutes (in a saucepan) until they have absorbed the colour and liquid completely.

Prepare the salad and add a little olive oil and seasoning. Using the remainder of olive oil, pour over the onions to blend with the cassis etc. Arrange salad in the centre of the plate.

Deep fry the brie until golden – approximately 3 minutes. Arrange cheese on top of leaves and dress with the onion, olive oil mixture around the cheese. Serve garnished with chervil.

Greg Robinson

Stuffed Courgettes With Parmesan And Pancetta

SERVES 4

4 large courgettes

1 tbsp olive oil

125g (4 oz) chopped pancetta

1 small onion, chopped

1 clove garlic, chopped

50g (2 oz) mushrooms, chopped

2 tbsp chopped black olives

2 tbsp sun-dried tomatoes, chopped

2 tbsp chopped basil

125g (4 oz) Mascarpone cheese

2 tbsp fresh grated Parmesan

salt and pepper

Preheat oven to 200°C/400°F/Gas Mark 6.

Trim courgettes and cut in half lengthways. Using a teaspoon, scoop out along the centre of the courgettes, and chop the removed flesh. Blanch the courgettes in boiling water for 3–4 minutes. Drain and cool.

Heat the oil in a frying pan and fry the pancetta for a few minutes to brown slightly before adding the onion and garlic. Continue to cook for a further 4 minutes, then stir in the chopped courgettes, the mushrooms, olives and sun-dried tomatoes, plus half the basil. Cook for a further 2 minutes before removing from the heat and stirring in the Mascarpone and most of the Parmesan. Add salt and pepper to taste.

Divide the filling among the courgettes, and place them side by side in a buttered dish. Sprinkle on the rest of the Parmesan and basil and cook in the oven for 15–20 minutes. Serve hot or cold.

Wild Mushroom, Asparagus And Potato Symphony

SERVES 4

12 asparagus spears

sprig of parsley

150ml (¼ pint) vegetable stock

125g (4 oz) wild mushrooms

12 cooked new potatoes

dash of cream

125g (4 oz) butter

salt and pepper

lemon juice

truffle oil, optional

Cook and refresh asparagus and parsley. Retain the cooking water.

Warm the stock, add mushrooms and new potatoes. Heat until hot right through and the mushrooms are cooked but still firm. Add a dash of cream and whisk in the butter.

Reheat asparagus in cooking water and then quickly drain and add to the potatoes in the butter sauce. Add parsley, season and adjust with lemon juice and a drizzle of truffle oil if using.

A Warm Salad Of Ciabatta Croutons With Bacon, Avocado And Vinaigrette Dressing

SERVES 4

4 slices ciabatta bread

2 tbsp olive oil

8 rashers smoked back bacon

250g (9 oz) cherry tomatoes

10 cos lettuce leaves (inside crisp heart leaves)

3 ripe avocados, peeled

4 eggs, soft boiled

2 tbsp fresh chives, chopped

Vinaigrette Dressing

5 tbsp extra virgin olive oil

2 tbsp white wine vinegar

1 tsp coarse-grain mustard

salt and freshly ground black pepper

Preheat the oven to 200°C/400°F/Gas Mark 6. Make the croutons: liberally brush the bread with olive oil on both sides, then cut into large cubes and bake in the preheated oven for approximately 10 minutes or until golden.

Make the dressing, put all the ingredients into a screw-top jar and shake vigorously until emulsified and slightly thickened.

Cut the bacon rashers into large strips and fry to crisp in a shallow pan, add the cherry tomatoes and warm through. Meanwhile, arrange the leaves on four serving plates. Add the crispy bacon and warm croutons to the salad. Slice the avocados over the leaves. Chop the egg into wedges and place on top. Deglaze the pan with the dressing and drizzle over the salad. Garnish with freshly chopped chives and serve immediately.

Red Pepper Mousse With Asparagus And Feta

SERVES 4

1 small onion

1 clove garlic

15g (¹/₂ oz) butter

1 large red pepper

300ml (¹/₂ pint) double cream

salt and ground black pepper

4 sprigs tarragon

1 egg

Asparagus and Feta

20 young asparagus spears

pinch of sugar

knob of butter

iced water

100g (3¹/₂ oz) feta cheese

¹/₂ small yellow pepper

6 black olives

Dressing

1 tbsp walnut oil

2 tsp extra virgin olive oil

1 tsp balsamic vinegar

¹/₂ level tsp caster sugar

salt and ground black pepper

Preheat oven to 140°C/275°F/Gas Mark 1. Lightly butter 4 dariole moulds or small ramekins.

Peel and finely chop onion. Peel and crush garlic. Melt butter in a small pan, add onion and garlic and cook until soft but not brown. Cut red pepper in half. Remove core, seed and membrane – you need 250g (9 oz) prepared weight. Chop pepper roughly. Add pepper to onion with cream. Cook until vegetables are soft. Season to taste. Purée in a blender or food processor. Rinse pan. Pass mixture through a fine sieve into clean pan. Strip leaves from tarragon and chop finely. Beat egg. Heat mixture gently. Add tarragon and beaten egg off the heat. Pour into prepared moulds and cover each one with foil. Place two folded muslin's or household cloths in a roasting tin. Sit moulds on cloths. Pour sufficient boiling water into tin to come half way up moulds. Bake in preheated oven for 1–1¹/₄ hours, until mousses are set. Leave to cool.

Prepare asparagus. Remove woody white ends of spears. Cut away stems, leaving just tips and about 5cm (2 inches) of stem. Use trimmings to make soup or to purée into a sauce. Bring a small pan of water to boiling point. Add asparagus tips, a pinch of sugar and a knob of butter. Cook for about 2 minutes, until just cooked but still crisp. Drain and refresh in iced water. Drain again. Dice feta cheese and yellow pepper. Stone olives and halve (or quarter if large).

Prepare dressing. Whisk oils, vinegar and sugar together in a bowl or small jug. Season to taste. Run a small sharp knife around mousses. Invert on to four serving plates, give a sharp shake to remove mousses from mould. Arrange asparagus around and scatter with feta, olives and pepper. Drizzle dressing over asparagus and cheese immediately before serving.

Paul Heathcote

Fricasse Of Artichokes

SERVES 1

4 sprigs parsley

2 cooked new potatoes

2 Jerusalem artichokes

¹/₂ leek

100ml (3¹/₂ fl. oz) vegetable stock or water

30g (1 oz) oyster mushrooms

1 tsp whipping cream

45g (1¹/₂ oz) butter

salt and pepper

lemon juice

Pick the heads from the parsley making sure no stalks remain. Cook in boiling salted water and refresh in cold water.

Cut potatoes and artichokes and leek into 2-cm-size (³/₄-inch) pieces and place in a pan with stock or water. Add the mushroom and cook until tender and very little liquid is left. Add cream and stir in butter. Add parsley. Season with salt, pepper and lemon juice.

Greg Robinson

Strawberry And Avocado Salad With A Fruit Dressing

SERVES 4

2 avocados

12–16 strawberries

2 slices smoked chicken breast (optional)

orange zest, long strands cut with a zester

Dressing

2 tbsp orange juice

1¹/₂ tbsp lemon juice

6 tbsp olive oil/sunflower oil mixed

Halve the avocados and remove the stones. Peel the fruit and slice. Arrange a fan of avocado slices on each of four plates. Reserve 4 strawberries and slice the remainder and arrange on top of the avocado.

If using the chicken breast, arrange the avocado and the chicken in an overlapping pattern with the strawberries on top. Sprinkle with strands of orange zest and garnish with the reserved whole strawberries.

To make the dressing, put all the ingredients in a screwtop jar. Fix the lid in position and shake well. Pour over the salad and serve.

Tessa Bramley

Fennel, Melon And Bean Salad With A Lemon Dressing

SERVES 4

½ small galia melon

2 handfuls baby spinach leaves

175g (6 oz) french beans

4 or 5 spring onions

1 handful small radishes

2 bulbs Florence fennel

1 tbsp freshly chopped chives

4 or 5 sprigs chervil, optional

Dressing

1 small lemon

1 fat clove of garlic

1 tsp caster sugar

5 tbsp extra virgin olive oil

salt and freshly ground black pepper

To make the dressing, squeeze the lemon into a bowl. Crush the clove of garlic and add to the lemon. Add all the other ingredients and whisk together. Leave for the flavours to infuse while preparing the salad ingredients.

Using a melon baller, cut the melon into balls or chop into neat cubes. Wash, pick and dry the spinach. Top, tail and blanch the beans. Peel and chop the spring onions. Top and tail the radishes. Cut in half. Prepare and chop the fennel, reserving the fronds to garnish the plate.

Sieve the dressing into a large bowl removing the pips and garlic. Stir in the chopped chives.

Put all the salad ingredients into the bowl with the dressing and toss lightly. Taste and adjust seasoning if necessary. Arrange the salad in the centre of 4 starter plates and top with sprigs of chervil. Garnish the plates with fennel fronds and serve chilled.

Mushroom Ravioli

SERVES 4

50g (2 oz) button or
field mushrooms

15g (¹/₂ oz) shiitake
mushrooms

1 small onion

2 sprigs tarragon

2 sprigs thyme

20g (³/₄ oz) butter,
more if needed

salt and pepper

300ml (¹/₂ pint)
whipping cream

3 roma tomatoes
diced

¹/₂ breast of chicken
puréed

sheet pasta (buy fresh
pasta sheets from
deli)

Wash and finely dice the mushrooms. Chop the onion and herbs. Melt the butter in a frying pan and cook the onion until soft. Add the mushrooms and herbs. When the mushrooms are cooked, stir in the cream and place on a tray to cool. When the mushrooms are cool. Squeeze out all the excess juice into a saucepan and season with salt and pepper and add chopped tomatoes and puréed chicken. Lay out the pasta sheets and place small spoonfuls of the mixture at evenly-spaced intervals (about 4cm/1¹/₂ inches apart) across and down the sheets. Dampen between the filling and place another sheet over the top, pressing down well around the spoonfuls of filling. Cut into squares and seal the edges by pressing with a fork. Place in the fridge for a few minutes. Cook in simmering boiling salted water for 4 minutes.

Tessa Bramley

Salad of Hazelnut-Coated Goats Cheese with a Redcurrant Dressing and a Mango Salsa

SERVES 4

1 bunch watercress or American cress

1 good handful of rocket leaves

1 few light green extra fine frisée leaves

125g (4 oz) hazelnuts

2 x 125g (4 oz) goats cheeses, British

2 tbsp hazelnut oil

Dressing

50g (2 oz) redcurrants, plus extra sprigs

1 tsp sugar

1 tbsp white wine vinegar

4 tbsp extra virgin olive oil

salt and pepper

Mango Salsa

1 mango, diced

6 spring onions, sliced

2 medium tomatoes, deseeded and diced

1 lime, juice and zest

1 red chilli, chopped

1 tsp caster sugar

few redcurrants

seasoning

Stir everything together for the salsa and taste for seasoning. Leave for the flavours to blend.

Wash and dry the salad leaves. Chill well.

Make the dressing. Liquidise everything together and taste for seasoning. Warm gently.

Either roast or toast the hazelnuts until the skins become papery and will rub off. Tip them into a tea towel and rub the skins off. Roughly chop the nuts.

Divide each cheese into 2. Reshape into rounds. Roll all sides in the chopped hazelnuts until well coated. Drizzle the surface with hazelnut oil and put to chill.

Preheat oven or grill. Oven temperature 220°C/450°F/Gas Mark 7. Heat a griddle pan or skillet until very hot. Cook goat's cheese on one side until golden brown. Turn carefully with a palette knife and cook the second side. It will take about 30 seconds each side. Remove to an oven tray and either bake or grill for 2–3 minutes until cheese is heated and slightly melted.

Arrange salad leaves on plates. Place hot cheese on top with a sprig of redcurrants. Drizzle the warm dressing over and around, allowing it to separate into golden and red pools. Add a spoonful of salsa to each plate and serve.

Pesto Orzo

SERVES 4

225g (8 oz) orzo, tiny rice-shaped pasta

salt, to taste

6 ripe tomatoes, diced

a few drops of balsamic vinegar

30g (1oz) pinenuts, lightly toasted in an un-greased pan

125g (4 oz) feta cheese, diced (preferably Greek sheep's milk)

sprigs of fresh basil, to garnish

250g (9 oz) mixed salad leaves

Pesto

75g (3 oz) basil leaves, chopped

6 tbsp olive oil

2 tbsp pecorino cheese, grated

3 tbsp walnuts, chopped

1 clove garlic, sliced

salt, to taste

Cook the orzo in boiling, salted water until it is *al dente*, then drain and leave to cool slightly.

To make the pesto, put the basil in a blender with the olive oil, cheese, walnuts and garlic. Blend until smooth, then season with salt. (This pesto can be used to garnish pizzas, soups and vegetable dishes. If it is too thick it can be thinned with additional olive oil.

Toss the pasta with 3–4 heaped tbsp of the pesto and set to one side.

Toss the tomatoes with the balsamic vinegar and salt.

Arrange the pasta on four serving plates next to a portion of tomatoes. Sprinkle the pinenuts over the pasta, and then sprinkle the whole dish with the feta cheese. Serve garnished with the basil sprigs on a bed of mixed Italian Salad.

Tessa Bramley

Tortellini Of Goats Cheese, Apricots And Cardamom With Mint Pesto

SERVES 8

350g (12 oz) saffron pasta (fresh from good delis or from your favourite recipe)

Filling

2 lemons

6 spring onions, finely chopped

1/2 sweet red pepper, finely diced

50g (2 oz) no-soak ready-to-eat dried apricots, finely chopped

12 green cardamom pods, seeds crushed

2 tbsp freshly chopped chives

350g (12 oz) soft lemony goats cheese such as Pantys Gawn or Roubilliac

salt and freshly ground black pepper

Mint Pesto

2 cloves of garlic, peeled

4 good bunches of mint, stalks removed

30g (1oz) pinenuts

1/2 tsp sugar

1 tbsp white wine vinegar

150ml (1/4 pint) extra virgin olive oil

Make pasta and put to rest. Prepare filling. Grate zest from lemon. Mix spring onions, red pepper, apricots, cardamom seeds, lemon zest, fresh chives and goats cheese. Season to taste.

Divide pasta into quarters. Roll out thinly or use pasta roller set at Number 6. Using a 6-cm (2 1/2-inch) plain tart cutter, cut out 5 circles per person. Put a teaspoon of the mixture on to half of the pasta circle. Moisten the edges with water and fold the pasta over the filling to form semi-circular shapes. Seal. Take the two ends and wrap right over left. Twist and turn the ends underneath to form a little hat shape. Repeat until you have 5 per portion. Stretch some cling film over a tray. Dust with flour and sit the tortellini on the film before chilling well to set the shapes.

Cook briefly in boiling salted water for about 2 minutes until cooked *al dente*. Drain well. Serve immediately with the mint pesto.

To make the mint pesto, purée all ingredients together in a blender or food processor until smooth. Season with salt and pepper to taste.

Mixed Vegetables In A Cider Cream Sauce With A Puff Pastry Case

SERVES 4

30g (1oz) butter

2 shallots, finely chopped

500ml (18 fl. oz) dry cider

500g (18 oz) mixed vegetables, cut into small florets or batons

2 tbsp crème fraîche

salt and fresh ground black pepper

400g (14 oz) puff pastry

150g (5 oz) cheddar cheese, grated

Melt the butter in a pan and fry the shallots until softened. Add the cider to the pan and bring gently to a boil. Put the vegetables in a steamer and steam over the cider until just cooked, but retaining a little crunch.

Boil the cider mixture down until you are left with 100ml (3$\frac{1}{2}$ fl. oz). Stir in the crème fraîche. Season to taste. Return the vegetables to the pan with the sauce.

Roll out the pastry to approximately 5mm ($\frac{1}{4}$ inch) in thickness and cut out 4 pieces measuring 15 x 8cm (6 x 3 inches). Sprinkle the pastry pieces with the cheese and bake for 15 to 20 minutes at 200°C/400°F/Gas Mark 6. Remove the pastry from the oven and allow to cool slightly before slicing in half horizontally. Spoon the vegetables on top of the bottom layer of pastry adding some of the cream sauce. Use the remaining pastry with the cheese to place on top of the dish.

Amanda Grant

Caerphilly Cheese And Caramelised Leek Tarts

SERVES 6

Pastry

225g (8 oz) plain flour

a pinch of salt

100g (3¹/₂ oz) unsalted butter

freshly ground black pepper

1 egg

1–2 tbsp milk

Filling

2 tbsp butter

2 tbsp olive oil

5 medium leeks, cleaned and cut into thin strips

3 tbsp Madeira sherry

salt and freshly ground black pepper

freshly chopped parsley

100g (3¹/₂ oz) Caerphilly cheese

Sift the flour and salt into a large bowl, rub in the butter until it resembles fine breadcrumbs and season with freshly ground black pepper. Beat the egg with the milk and work enough into the mix to form a dough. Wrap in cling film and leave to rest for at least 30 minutes.

For the filling, melt the butter and heat the oil in a large-based frying pan over a medium heat. Add the leeks and cook, stirring until soft. Reduce the heat to low and cook, stirring occasionally, for 25 minutes or until the leeks have caramelised. Stir in the Madeira and continue to cook, stirring for 4 minutes or until soft. Put to one side.

Roll out the pastry to 5mm (¹/₄ inch) and line six 8-cm (3-inch) flan tins, trim the edges and prick the base. Refrigerate for 10 minutes.

Preheat the oven to 180°C/350°F/Gas Mark 4. Line the pastry cases with greaseproof paper and beans and bake for 15 minutes, remove paper and beans and bake for a further 10 minutes.

Remove from the tins and place on a baking sheet. Preheat the grill to medium. Spoon the leeks into the pastry cases, season with salt, freshly ground black pepper and lots of freshly chopped parsley. Crumble the Caerphilly cheese over the top and put under the preheated grill for 2 minutes or until the cheese has melted.

Serve hot with a fresh salad.

Roasted Tomato, Cream Cheese And Basil Tarts

SERVES 4

150g (5 oz) baby yellow tomatoes

150g (5 oz) cherry tomatoes

150g (5 oz) baby plum tomatoes

7 tbsp olive oil

salt and freshly ground black pepper

350g (12 oz) puff pastry

175g (6 oz) cream cheese, beaten

50g (2 oz) freshly torn basil

Preheat the oven to 220°C/425°F/Gas Mark 7. Place the tomatoes on a greased baking sheet. Drizzle with 5 tbsp olive oil, season with salt and freshly ground black pepper and cook in the preheated oven for 15 minutes.

Roll out the pastry to about 5mm ($1/4$ inch) thick. Cut four 10-cm (4 inch) squares. Cut a 1-cm ($1/3$-inch) border along two sides of each square, leaving 1-cm ($1/3$-inch) gaps at each end. Repeat the remaining sides so that you have two 'L'-shaped cuts (i.e. two opposite corners have a 2-cm ($2/3$-inch) piece of uncut pastry). Lift up the points of the loose corners and pass under each other, moisten the overlapping pastry and prick the centre. Place on greased baking sheets and leave to rest for 30 minutes in the refrigerator.

Divide the cream cheese among the four pastry cases, half of the torn basil and season with salt and freshly ground black pepper. Top with the roasted tomatoes and cook the tarts in the preheated oven for 30 minutes or until the pastry is golden brown and puffed.

Drizzle with remaining olive oil and scatter over the remaining freshly torn basil. Serve immediately.

Amanda Grant

Wild Mushroom Stew On Toasted Brioche

SERVES 4

30g (1oz) dried
    Porcini slices

225g (8 oz) field
    mushrooms

225g (8 oz) chestnut
    mushrooms

1 tbsp olive oil

30g (1oz) butter

¹/₂ clove garlic, peeled
    and chopped

2 tbsp parsley,
    roughly chopped

2 sprigs oregano

2 drops Tabasco

2 tbsps Madeira

1 tsp softened butter
    mixed with 1 tsp
    plain flour (beurre
    manie)

4 slices brioche,
    toasted

Pour 250ml (9 fl. oz) very hot water over the dried Porcini mushrooms and leave to infuse for at least 30 minutes, preferably one hour. Lift the slices out of the bowl and squeeze over the bowl so as not to waste any of the flavoured juices.

Chop the Porcini into large bite-size pieces, chop the field and chestnut mushrooms into similarly-sized pieces.

Heat the oil and butter in a frying pan, add the Porcini and gently cook for 3 minutes. Add the other mushrooms and cook over a high heat for 5 minutes. Add the garlic, herbs and Tabasco. Cook for another minute, before adding the Madeira and Porcini liquor, reduce to about half. Add the beurre manie and stir until the stew has thickened slightly.

Serve immediately on top of the brioche slices.

Chilli And Parmesan Popovers With A Chunky Tomato Sauce

SERVES 4

Popovers
2 large eggs
175ml (6 fl. oz) milk
4 tbsp water
100g (3¹/₂ oz) plain flour
¹/₄ tsp salt
1 red chilli, deseeded and finely chopped
¹/₈ tsp cayenne pepper
60g (2¹/₂ oz) Parmesan, finely grated

Sauce
900g (2 lb) ripe tomatoes
2 tbsp olive oil
¹/₂ small onion, peeled and finely chopped
salt and freshly ground black pepper
¹/₂ tsp sugar
2 spring onions, roughly chopped
1 fresh red chilli pepper, deseeded and finely chopped
2 tbsp freshly chopped coriander
2 tbsp fresh lemon juice

Preheat the oven to 200°C/400°F/Gas Mark 6. Bake the tomatoes for 6–10 minutes. When the tomatoes are cool enough to handle, core and peel off their skins. Reduce the oven temperature to 190°C/375°F/Gas Mark 5 and grease 12 small muffin tins.

Whisk together the eggs, milk and water. Add the flour, salt, chilli and cayenne. Whisk until combined, ignoring any lumps.

Spoon half the mixture into the tins, sprinkle half of the cheese over the top and divide the rest of the batter among the tins. Top with the remaining cheese, bake for 25 minutes in the middle of the oven, until firm. Cut small slits in the top of each and return to the oven for a further 5–10 minutes or until golden.

While the popovers are cooking, finish the tomato sauce. Roughly purée the tomatoes in a food processor. Heat the oil in a frying pan and gently sauté the onions until soft and translucent. Add the puréed tomatoes and cook until they have thickened and the excess liquid has evaporated. Taste and season with salt, freshly ground black pepper and the sugar. Add the spring onions, chilli pepper, coriander and lemon juice to the tomatoes and mix together well.

Serve 2 to 3 popovers to each person with the chunky sauce, for a perfect starter or light snack.

Jean Davies

Cheese And Onion And Mixed Herb Bread

MAKES 2 LOAVES
675g (1¹/₂ lb) strong white bread flour

2 tsp salt

2 tsp sugar

2 x 6g pkts dried yeast

5 tbsp olive oil

75g (3 oz) Cheddar cheese, grated

1 medium onion, diced

1 tbsp fresh rosemary

1 tbsp fresh thyme

1 tbsp fresh parsley

finely sliced onion

sea salt

Sieve flour, salt, sugar and dried yeast into a large bowl. Add the olive oil to about 125ml (4 fl. oz) warm water and mix this into the flour to form a dough. Knead until shiny. This bread does not require a lot of kneading (contrary to popular belief).

Put the dough in a lightly oiled bowl, and cover with a clean tea towel. Put the dough in a warm place to rise until it has doubled in bulk – approximately 40–60 minutes.

When the dough has risen, divide into two halves. To one half add the grated cheese and chopped onion. Mix well into the dough and shape into an oval. To the other half of the dough add the freshly chopped herbs. Top both loaves with finely sliced onion and sprinkle with sea salt.

Leave the two loaves to rise for a further 40 minutes. Meanwhile preheat the oven to 230°C/450°F/Gas Mark 8. When dough has risen, place each loaf on a greased baking tray. Bake for 10 minutes then spray with water, and bake for a further 20–25 minutes until golden brown. Remove from the oven and cool on wire racks, serve warm or cold.

Honey-Roasted Duck Salad – Teriyaki

SERVES 2

250g (9 oz) rocket leaves

1 head lollo rosso

4 tsp runny honey

2 tsp cooking oil

1 tsp paprika pepper

salt and pepper

2 breast of Barbary duck

150ml (¼ pint) soy sauce

3 tbsp sake or white wine vinegar

2.5cm (1 inch) square of fresh root ginger, shredded

1 lime

2 red chillies, chopped

fresh coriander

1 tsp olive oil

fresh chervil, for salad garnish

Wash leaves and reserve. Melt half the honey in a hot frying pan with the cooking oil and paprika.

Season the duck breast and score with a sharp knife. Sear the duck breast in the honey mixture until golden (2 minutes – skin side into the pan) and turnover and sear other side. Put duck breast in hot oven at 220°C/425°F/Gas Mark 7 on a baking tray for 7 minutes, remove and allow to rest.

While it is cooking, prepare the sauce. Mix together the soy, remaining honey, sake, root ginger and juice of lime and chopped chilli. Heat the sauce to infuse all flavours (in a saucepan) and finally add chopped coriander.

Arrange leaves on plate and dress with a little olive oil and season. Carve duck breast into thin slices and arrange around leaves. Pour the sauce over the duck and serve, garnished with chervil.

Tessa Bramley

Salad Of Calves Liver With An Aromatic Beetroot Dressing

SERVES 4

selection of mixed colour and flavour salad leaves – e.g. escarole, rocket, cos

30g (1oz) unsalted butter

225g (8 oz) calves liver, thinly sliced, skinned and trimmed of all veins and sinew

2 tbsp Amontillado sherry

handful of freshly chopped chives

Beetroot Dressing

1 small cooked beetroot

2 tbsp white chicken stock

2 sprigs fresh thyme, stalks removed

4 tbsp extra virgin olive oil

1 tbsp balsamic vinegar

1 tsp pink peppercorns

salt and freshly ground black pepper

Make dressing. Liquidise beetroot with stock. Heat gently in saucepan with all remaining ingredients. Whisk well and check seasoning. Heat gently but do not boil. The dressing will separate slightly on the plate to make a beautiful golden and red marbled effect.

Wash and dry salad leaves. Season and arrange on plates.

Heat a cast iron pan or skillet until very hot. Swirl in butter and fry liver briskly about 1 minute each side only – it should still be pink in the middle. Remove liver and add sherry to pan, scraping up all the buttery sediment to make a sauce. Arrange liver neatly around the salad, pouring the sauce over the liver. Pour the beetroot dressing lightly over and around the salad and liver. Sprinkle with the chives.

Chicken With Herbs Wrapped In Prosciutto Ham

SERVES 4

2 tbsp plain flour

2 tsp fines herbs

1¹/₂ tsp ground black pepper

2 chicken breasts

8 slices prosciutto ham

50g (2 oz) butter

1 tbsp olive oil

4–6 tbsp Marsala

4 tbsp fresh grated Parmesan

Mix the flour, herbs and black pepper together and sprinkle on a plate.

Skin the chicken breasts and place them between 2 sheets of cling film or baking parchment. Using a rolling pin or similar beat the chicken breasts until they are twice their original size. Cut each breast in half, producing 4 portions. Wrap each piece of chicken in 2 pieces of prosciutto ham and then press into the flour mixture.

Melt the butter and add the oil to a frying pan. Gently fry the chicken for 2–3 minutes on each side. Pour the Marsala into the pan and let it bubble briefly before sprinkling each piece of chicken with some grated cheese. Baste with a little of the pan juices before covering the pan and continuing cooking for a few minutes to allow the cheese to melt. If you would like to develop the herb flavours even more, add more of the dried herb mixture to the cheese.

Amanda Grant

Marinated Wasabi Beef With Tempura Vegetable Jumble

SERVES 4

4 small beef steaks

freshly ground black pepper

4 tsp wasabi paste (Japanese variety of horseradish)

6 tbsp sake

2 tbsp caster sugar

2 tbsp fresh pink ginger or fresh root ginger, finely sliced

soy sauce, to serve

Tempura Batter Mix

200ml (7 fl. oz) water

1 egg

100g (3¹/₂ oz) plain flour

50g (2 oz) cornflour

Tempura Vegetables

1 courgette

¹/₂ small aubergine, halved lengthways

1 carrot, peeled and trimmed

2 spring onions, trimmed

vegetable oil, for frying

Rub the steaks very generously with the pepper and place them under a hot grill for 4 to 5 minutes on each side. Leave to rest for 10 minutes before slicing into thin strips. Mix together the wasabi paste, sake, sugar and finely sliced pink ginger or fresh root ginger and spoon over the beef strips.

Make the tempura vegetable jumble: mix together the water and egg and chill. Cut all of the vegetables into strips, 8cm (3 inches) long and 3 mm (¹/₈ inch) wide. Put the courgette, aubergine and carrot in a colander and sprinkle with salt. Leave for 30 minutes and then rinse thoroughly under cold water, add the spring onions. Preheat a pan of vegetable oil, quickly mix together all of the batter ingredients, ignoring any lumps. Using your hands, dip the vegetables into the batter and make sure the batter and vegetables are combined to form one gluey mass.

Scoop a large tablespoonful of mixture into the preheated oil and cook, turning halfway, for approximately 3 minutes or until golden brown. Drain on kitchen paper.

To serve, place the tempura vegetable jumble on 4 serving plates, top with the marinated wasabi beef and serve with soy sauce.

A Salad Of Sautéed Oatmeal Mussels With A Whisky And Lemon Dressing

SERVES 4

20 green shell mussels, scrubbed and closed

30g (1oz) clarified butter

2 leeks, cut into thick ribbons and blanched

200g (7oz) baby spinach leaves, washed and dried

salt and pepper

50g (2 oz) oatmeal, toasted

Dressing
4 tbsp whisky

1 lemon, juice

2 tbsp fresh parsley, very finely chopped

freshly ground black pepper

sea salt

Cook the mussels, place them in a pan with a couple of tablespoons of water, cover and cook over a high heat until all the mussels open, approximately 5 minutes.

Heat half the butter in a frying pan. Add the leeks and spinach and warm through until the spinach wilts. Season. Divide among four warm bowls.

Quickly sauté the cooked mussels in the remaining butter until they are hot. Spoon over the warm vegetables. (If you have the mussel shells, these can be used to decorate the plates).

Add the whisky to the pan, boiling rapidly and scraping sediment from the bottom of the pan. Add the lemon juice, parsley, salt and pepper. Pour over the mussels. Sprinkle with toasted oatmeal. Serve immediately.

Greg Robinson

Salt Cod Brandade

SERVES 4

750g (1lb 10 oz) salt cod

300ml (1/2 pint) olive oil

250ml (9 fl. oz) milk

2 cloves garlic, chopped

1/2 tsp lemon juice

pinch of nutmeg

pinch of white pepper

French bread croutes, fried in olive oil and then rubbed with garlic

finely chopped parsley to garnish

Soak the salt cod in cold water for 2 days, changing the water several times. Drain the cod and put it into a pan of cold water just to cover. Bring to the boil and then poach over a low heat for 8 to 10 minutes until just tender. Drain the fish and allow to cool slightly before flaking with a fork and discarding all the skin and bone.

Heat the oil in a saucepan until very hot. Scald the milk in another saucepan. Put the fish into a food processor and add the hot oil a little at a time, pulsing the processor rather than mixing continuously. The mixture should not be overworked or it will become too soft and lack texture. When the oil has been added, continue with the milk, once again adding the liquid a little at a time. The finished purée should be white, smooth and stiff enough to hold its shape.

Stir in the garlic, lemon juice, nutmeg and pepper before spooning the mixture into separate bowls and surrounding with the croutes. Sprinkle with chopped parsley.

Greg Robinson

Spanish-Style Baked Fish

SERVES 4

4 portions of haddock fillet

1/2 tsp salt

1/2 tsp ground paprika

1/2 tsp cayenne pepper

1/2 tsp nutmeg

2-3 tbsp olive oil

1 medium onion, thinly sliced

2 cloves garlic, crushed

2 tbsp pimento, chopped

125g (4 oz) ham, finely chopped

8 anchovy fillets, soaked in milk

8 slices tomato

2 tbsp chopped chives

4 mushrooms, sliced

2 glasses dry Spanish wine

melted butter, to finish

Wash and dry the fish fillets. Mix the salt and spices together and rub into the fish.

Heat the olive oil in an ovenproof skillet and lightly brown the onions and garlic. Add the pimento and ham and cook for a further 5 minutes before adding the fish fillets. Cook for a couple of minutes and then turn the fish over.

Lay 2 soaked anchovy fillets on each fillet of fish, and then add 2 slices of tomato, the chopped chives and the sliced mushrooms. Pour on the wine and cover the pan. The dish should bake in the oven at 190°C/375°F/Gas Mark 5 for 20-25 minutes. The contents of the pan will become rather dry, so if necessary add a splash more wine. However the dish is dry, so only add more wine to prevent burning. Serve with a small salad and drizzle melted butter over the fish.

Aaron Patterson

Fish Kebab With Tomato Sauce

SERVES 4

600g (1lb 5 oz) fresh
  fish (may include
  monkfish, fresh
  tuna, tiger prawns)

2 limes

salt and pepper

150ml ($^1/_4$ pint) olive
  oil

$^1/_2$ red pepper

$^1/_2$ yellow pepper

$^1/_2$ Spanish onion

a little balsamic
  vinegar

Tomato Sauce
200g (7 oz) tomatoes

$^1/_2$ red chilli, deseeded

1 clove garlic, crushed

1 pinch cayenne
  pepper

4 leaves of basil,
  chopped

Dice the fish into 3cm (1$^1/_4$ inch) cubes. Peel the prawns. Squeeze the limes. Season the fish with salt and pepper and marinate for $^1/_2$ hour in the lime juice and olive oil.

Peel the peppers, deseed and dice (same size as the fish). Save any of the trimmings for the sauce. Peel and cube the onion. Soften the peppers and onion in a little hot olive oil. Season and deglaze the pan with some balsamic vinegar. Place the softened vegetables, fish and prawns on skewers and cook on the barbecue (or grill).

Roast the tomatoes, pepper trimmings, chilli, garlic together. Purée and sieve. Season with cayenne, salt and pepper and add the chopped basil. This sauce can be served hot or cold with the fish kebabs.

Spicy Moussaka Of Fresh Tuna

SERVES 4

1 aubergine, cut into
wafer-thin slices

vegetable oil for
frying

225g (8 oz) fresh
tuna fish

8 slices sun-dried
tomatoes

fresh coriander leaves,
to garnish

pinch of ground
cinnamon

pinch of paprika
pepper

Tomato Sauce
2 cloves garlic

1 onion, sliced

450g (1lb) tomatoes,
deseeded and
skinned

2 red chillies

olive oil

white wine, to taste

Fry the aubergine slices until crisp in a saucepan of hot oil at 170°C/325°F. Drain on kitchen towel.

Griddle (or pan sear) wafer-thin slices of fresh tuna for 20 seconds each side and reserve.

Prepare the sauce by sweating garlic and onion. Add tomatoes and chillies, cook for 20 minutes and put through a food processor.

Construct the dish by layering one slice of aubergine and one slice of sun-dried tomato, some coriander and a slice of fresh tuna. Season with cinnamon and paprika and repeat process to form a tall stack. Finish the sauce with a little olive oil and white wine, to taste and spoon around. Garnish with coriander.

Steven Saunders

Fish Cakes With Salad And Strawberry Vinegar

SERVES 4

200g (7 oz) can tuna fish

2 large potatoes, cooked and mashed

2 egg yolks

1 small bunch of chives

2 tbsp grated mild Cheddar cheese

6 tbsp breadcrumbs

1 egg

dash of milk

3 tbsp flour

salt

vegetable oil, for frying

1 iceberg lettuce

1 curly endive

Dressing

2 tsp icing sugar

100ml (3 1/2 fl. oz) white wine vinegar

125g (4 oz) strawberries, puréed

Mix the tuna, mashed potato, egg yolks, chives, cheese and 1 tablespoon of breadcrumbs together.

Mix the egg, milk and a pinch salt together. Line up the flour, egg mix, and breadcrumbs in bowls in front of you. Roll the tuna mix into shapes and coat in flour, egg and breadcrumbs. Fry over a gentle heat in a little vegetable oil until golden brown on both sides.

While frying, blend the icing sugar, vinegar and puréed strawberries together, for the dressing. Arrange washed leaves in the centre of a plate. Spoon over the dressing and place the fish cake on top.

Pot Au Feu Of Scallops

SERVES 4

12 king scallops

vegetable oil

100ml (3¹/₂ fl. oz) sweet white wine

salt and pepper

4 portions fresh spinach pasta noodles

50g (2 oz) butter

chopped chives

chopped fresh coriander

Nage

1 onion, sliced

1 leek, sliced

2 stalks celery, chopped

2 carrots, chopped

¹/₂ head garlic

2 lemon, thinly sliced

1 sprig fresh coriander

1 sprig tarragon

200ml (7 fl. oz) dry white wine

In a very hot frying pan heat a little vegetable oil and sear the scallops till crisp on one side, about 2–3 minutes. Turn over and seal and remove pan from heat.

Put all the ingredients for the 'nage' in a large pan with 1 litre (1³/₄ pints). Add the sweet wine and season.

Blanch the spinach noodles and drain. Boil the butter with 3 tbsp water to make an emulsion. Add the chopped chives and add the noodles to this.

Serve noodles piled in the centre of a serving bowl or individual bowls with 3 scallops around and the 'nage juices', finished with fresh chopped coriander.

Tessa Bramley

Creamy Seafood Risotto

SERVES 4

24 mussels

24 Venus clams – or
fresh cockles

150ml ('/₄ pint) white
wine

300ml ('/₂ pint) fish
stock

24 fresh shrimp – or
8 Dublin Bay
prawns

1 small onion, finely
chopped

1 clove garlic, crushed

3 tbsp olive oil

50g (2 oz)
mushrooms, finely
sliced

175g (6 oz) risotto
rice

2 tsp lemon juice

salt and pepper

1 tbsp chopped
parsley

1 tbsp chopped
fennel leaf

Wash and de-beard all the shellfish. Heat wine
with 150ml ('/₄ pint) water in a wide-based pan
and tip in the mussels and clams. Shake over a
high heat until the shells open (this will take
seconds). Remove the shellfish. Take the meat
from the shells. Pass the cooking liquor through a
fine sieve and add it to the fish stock. Peel the
shrimp or prawns.

Fry the onion and garlic in 2 tbsp oil until
softened. Add mushrooms and rice and stir until
all rice is coated with oil. Add some of the fish
stock and lemon juice. Reduce the heat to simmer
and gently cook the rice. Season lightly. Keep
shaking the pan and adding a little more stock as
it is needed. The risotto should not be allowed to
become dry or to stick to the pan but should
retain a creaminess about it. The whole process
will take about 20 minutes. Keep testing the rice
– it should not be mushy. The grains should be
firm without any hard white bits in the middle.
When it is cooked the liquid will have almost
been absorbed with a cream residue surrounding
the rice.

Stir fry the prawns in the remaining olive oil
until they turn pink. Add cooked mussels and
clams to the rice mixture, heat through and stir in
the chopped herbs and cooked prawns. Adjust
seasoning. Serve either with a sprinkling of herbs
on top, or, better still, with shavings of Parmesan
cheese (a potato peeler does this quite well).

Sorrel, Rocket and Watercress Salad with Char-Griddled Wild Salmon with an Elderflower Dressing

SERVES 4

6 radishes, thinly
   sliced

1 bunch watercress

1 bunch rocket

1 ripe pear, peeled,
   cored and thinly
   sliced

a good handful of
   French sorrel leaves

2 heads chive flowers

Dressing

1 tbsp elderflower
   cordial

1 tsp white wine
   vinegar

4 tbsp extra virgin
   olive oil

salt and pepper, to
   taste

Salmon

350g (12 oz) fillet of
   wild salmon

2 tbsp extra virgin
   olive oil

salt and freshly
   ground black
   pepper

Heat a griddle. Preheat oven to 220°C/450°F/Gas Mark 7.

Put dressing ingredients into a screwtop jar and shake well or whisk together.

Prepare salad ingredients. Put into bowl and season very lightly.

Cut up salmon into small pieces. Season. Drizzle top surface with oil. Put salmon on griddle, oil side down and allow to form a golden crust. Remove with palette knife, and bake in oven for 4 to 5 minutes, golden-side uppermost until just cooked. It should still be pink in the middle.

Dress salad and arrange on plates. Top with cooked salmon and drizzle a little dressing over. Scatter with chive flowers and serve.

Tessa Bramley

Griddled Fresh Sardines With A Chilli, Lemon And Marjoram Dressing

SERVES 4

fresh sardines

1 lemon, zest and juice

8 tbsp extra virgin olive oil

sea salt

freshly ground black pepper

1 red chilli, deseeded and finely chopped

6 spring onions, prepared and thinly sliced

1 handful fresh marjoram or oregano

1 tsp caster sugar

1 lemon, cut into wedges

4 stoned black olives

4 sprigs flat leaf parsley

olive bread, to serve

Scale, gut and dehead the sardines. Wash and dry.

Whisk together the lemon zest and juice, oil and seasonings. Add the prepared chilli, spring onions and marjoram leaves picked from the stems. Season the sardines and pop a few leaves of marjoram inside the gut. Put into a dish and pour the marinade over them. Leave in the fridge for a couple of hours if possible, but at least for 1 hour.

Preheat a griddle, ridged cast iron pan or the grill. Remove the fish from the marinade, draining off juices and then throw on the hot griddle to cook. After about 2 minutes when the fish is opaque on that side, turn the sardines and cook on the second side for another 2 minutes or so – taking care not to over cook them.

Meanwhile, heat up the marinade with the sugar added to serve as a dressing with the fish. Taste and adjust seasoning if necessary. Serve sardines on hot plates with a little of the dressing poured over, a wedge of lemon, a black olive and some flat leaf parsley. Also serve some warm Portuguese olive bread to mop up the juices – this will complete the dish.

Casserole Of Bream And King Prawns With Bok Choy, Shiitaki Mushrooms, Noodles, Coriander And Ginger

SERVES 2

fresh ginger

1 fillet of bream, cut into 2 pieces

2 king prawns

50g (2 oz) Chinese noodles

200ml (7 fl. oz) vegetable stock

2 shiitaki mushrooms

1 spring onion, sliced

4 leaves boy choy, cooked

chopped coriander

salt, to taste

Peel the ginger by scraping with a spoon. Slice and cut into fine strips.

Steam the bream and prawns in a basket. Cook noodles in boiling salted water. Place in a large serving bowl.

Meanwhile bring stock to the boil with sliced shiitaki mushrooms and spring onion, add the bok choy, coriander and ginger. Season with salt. Arrange fish and vegetables on noodles and pour over the stock.

Greg Robinson

Watercress Roulade With Prawns

SERVES 4

60g (2¹/₂ oz) butter

50g (2 oz) plain flour

250ml (9 fl. oz) milk

60g (2¹/₂ oz)
Parmesan cheese,
grated

4 eggs, separated

500g (18 oz)
watercress

small punnet of
raspberries

Filling

250g (9 oz) cream
cheese

6 tbsp sour cream

250g (9 oz) prawns,
chopped

Heat the butter in a pan. Add the flour and cook for a minute. Gradually add the milk, stirring constantly over the heat until the mixture boils and thickens. Remove from the heat and add the cheese, egg yolks and chopped watercress. Transfer the mixture to a large bowl. Beat the egg whites until they form soft peaks, and fold them lightly into the watercress mixture. Pour the mixture into a greased and lined swiss roll tin 25 x 30cm (10 x 12 inch) and bake at 190°C/375°F/Gas Mark 5 for 20 minutes or until the roulade is golden brown.

Whilst the roulade is cooking, mix together the cream cheese and the sour cream. Stir in the chopped prawns. When the roulade is cooked, quickly turn it out on to a wire rack covered with a tea towel. Carefully remove the lining paper and spread with the cream cheese mixture. Roll up the roulade using the tea towel to help roll from the short side. Decorate with raspberries to serve.

Serve with a home-made mayonnaise made with raspberry vinegar, and some crushed (and sieved) raspberries lightly folded into the sauce leaving swirls of colour.

Spiced Prawns

SERVES 4

2 tbsp sesame oil

675g (1¹/₂ lb)
  uncooked prawns,
  shelled and
  deveined – tails on

3 spring onions, white
  part chopped, green
  part thinly sliced
  and kept separate

2 tsp grated root
  ginger

150ml (¹/₄ pint) fish
  stock

2 tbsp tomato purée

2 tbsp dry sherry

2 tbsp cider vinegar

¹/₂ tsp cayenne pepper

Chinese rice, cooked
  to serve

2 tbsp lightly toasted
  sesame seeds
  (optional)

Heat 1 tbsp of oil in a wok. Stir fry the prawns over a moderate heat for 2 minutes. Spoon the prawns into a dish. Add the rest of the oil to the wok and stir fry the white of the onions and the ginger for 30 seconds. Stir in the stock, tomato purée, sherry, vinegar and cayenne pepper.

Simmer for 3 minutes. Return the prawns to the pan and continue cooking for a further 3 minutes, stirring frequently. Sprinkle half of the green parts of the onions on the dish and pour into a bowl. Cool and refrigerate for several hours.

Serve some rice in the bottom of individual bowls. Spoon the prawns and sauce over the rice and sprinkle with the remaining green onions and sesame seeds, if using.

Main Courses
Fish & Shellfish

Aaron Patterson

Pan-Fried Fillet Of Salmon With Spinach And Tomato Sauce

SERVES 4

4 x 50g (2 oz) pieces of salmon

250g (9 oz) tomatoes (sweet cherry ones are best)

8 tbsp olive oil plus extra for frying

4 good handfuls of sorrell leaves

1 tsp balsamic vinegar

50g (2 oz) unsalted butter, diced

10 picked basil leaves

salt and pepper

Liquidise the tomatoes with the 8 tbsp olive oil, balsamic vinegar, salt and pepper. Sieve into a pan and warm gently. Whisk in the butter but do not boil.

Fry the salmon until golden brown and allow to rest. At the last moment, wilt the sorrel in the pan with the salmon and add the sauce. Serve with asparagus and new potatoes.

Herb-Crusted Salmon On Puy Lentils With A Red Wine Sauce

SERVES 4

Marinade

2 sprigs tarragon, finely chopped with stems reserved

2 sprigs flat-leaf parsley, finely chopped with stems reserved

a bunch of chives, finely chopped

3 tbsp rock salt

1 tbsp sugar

zest of 1 lemon

freshly ground black pepper

6 skinless salmon fillets (approximately 200g (7 oz) each)

Lentils

350g (12 oz) puy lentils, rinsed

2 carrots, peeled and diced

2 sticks celery, diced

1 small onion, finely chopped

2 cloves garlic, peeled and chopped

4 sprigs thyme

1/2 tsp rock salt

In a small bowl, mix the tarragon, parsley, chives, salt, sugar, zest and freshly ground black pepper. Spread on to both sides of the salmon fillets and marinate at room temperature for at least one hour before starting to cook the lentils.

Cover the lentils with 850ml (1 1/2 pints) water, bring to a simmer, reduce the heat to low. Cover and simmer for 15 minutes. Add all the other ingredients except the salt, cover and cook for 15 minutes. Add the salt and cook for 5 minutes. Stand for 5 minutes with the lid on, keep an eye on them and serve immediately, so that they do not have the chance to go mushy.

To make the sauce, put the red wine, port, red wine vinegar, shallots and herb stems into a saucepan. Bring to the boil and reduce to approximately 100ml (3 1/2 fl. oz). Strain into a clean saucepan, put to one side.

Preheat the oven to 180°C/350°F/Gas Mark 4. Brush the herb and salt marinade off the salmon. Lightly oil a heavy skillet or griddle pan and heat until very hot. Sear the fillets on both sides until lightly browned, approximately 1 minute on each side. Transfer to a baking sheet and cook in the preheated oven for 7–10 minutes.

Sauce

- 300ml ('/2 pint) red wine
- 100ml (3'/2 fl. oz) port
- 3 tbsp red wine vinegar
- 2 shallots, peeled and minced
- 100g (3'/2 oz) unsalted butter, chilled and diced

Bring the sauce back to the boil, then reduce the heat. Gradually whisk in the butter without boiling, season with salt and freshly ground black pepper. To serve, spoon the lentils into the middle of the serving plates, place the salmon on top and spoon the sauce around the lentils.

Paul Heathcote

Butterfly Prawns With Chilli And Garlic And Rocket Salad

SERVES 4

- 40 Tiger prawns
- 1 red chilli pepper
- 1 clove garlic
- olive oil
- juice of '/2 lemon
- 1 shallot, finely diced
- sea salt
- 500g (18 oz) rocket salad leaves

Prepare the prawns by cutting them down the back to 'butterfly' them. Split the chilli in half, deseed and dip in water – this helps to reduce some of the fieriness of the chilli. Chop finely. Chop the garlic and place in a tray with chilli, a generous drizzling of olive oil, lemon juice and shallots. Season with sea salt. Marinate the prawns by laying them flat in the oil for about one hour.

Grill on a barbecue for about 2–3 minutes, taking care not to overcook them. Serve with rocket salad.

Navarin Of Salmon

SERVES 4

2 cloves garlic

2 shallots

225g (8 oz) unsalted butter

sprig of fresh thyme

salt and pepper

500g (18 oz) mussels in their shells (or New Zealand green lip)

150ml (¼ pint) white wine

500g (18 oz) salmon fillet (pin boned andskinned)

200g (7 oz) fresh spinach noodles

1 tsp olive oil

fresh coriander, chopped

fresh tarragon, chopped

fresh chives, chopped

2–3 tomatoes, chopped

Finely chop the garlic and shallots. Add 50g (2 oz) of butter to approximately 600 ml (1 pint) of boiling water in a shallow sauté-style pan. Add the garlic, shallot and thyme into this liquor and season.

Clean, wash and debeard the mussels, removing all the barnacles. Heat up a frying pan until smoking hot, add the mussels to this pan and immediately a good 150ml (¼ pint) of white wine.

While mussels are cooking, poach the salmon pieces in the water, butter and thyme liquor. Cover the salmon with a butter wrapper or a piece of greaseproof paper and turn the pan down to a simmer for approximately 5–6 minutes.

Cook noodles in a saucepan of boiling water with a little olive oil and seasoning. Cook for 2–3 minutes and drain. Make a tower (using a fork) of the pasta and serve in the centre of a deep bowl.

Add the remainder of the butter to the mussels and more white wine if necessary and then the chopped herbs and tomatoes. Serve the salmon around the pasta with the mussels scattered around and the sauce over.

Tessa Bramley

Griddled King Scallops With Crispy Chinese Vegetables

SERVES 2

10 king scallops (cleaned)

1 tbsp olive oil

1/2 red chilli, finely chopped

1 stem lemon grass, inner part finely sliced

1 clove garlic, crushed

6 asparagus spears, sliced across at an angle

5cm (2 inch) piece of mooli, peeled and sliced

6 spring onions, sliced

16 broad beans, blanched and peeled

16 snow peas or mangetout, sliced across at an angle

2 baby pak choi, stems sliced or leaves torn

1/2 yellow pepper, cut into chunks

1 piece stem ginger, cut into julienne

1/2 lime, juice only

1 tbsp sesame oil

dash of Kikoman soy sauce

Dressing

1 lime, finely grated zest of whole lime and juice of 1/2 the lime

3 tsp ginger syrup from stem ginger

1 tbsp olive oil

Caramelised Pecans

2 tbsp sugar

dash of water

knob of unsalted butter

10 pecan nuts

1 tbsp toasted sesame seeds

Preheat oven to 220°C/425°F/Gas Mark 7. Gently heat wok to all over even heat. Heat griddle or skillet.

Add sugar and water to small pan. Heat to golden. Add butter and nuts. Swirl to coat. Remove to baking parchment. Sprinkle with sesame seeds. Allow to cool and crisp.

Griddle scallops until golden on one side. Remove and place on oven tray golden side up. Combine dressing ingredients and drizzle over. Heat for 1 minute ONLY in oven until hot.

Add oil to wok and stir fry all vegetables, starting with chilli, lemon grass, garlic and asparagus. Add rest of vegetables and seasonings. Taste and adjust. Stir in nuts and finally scallops. Serve in a pretty dish.

Salad Of Roasted Scallops With Crispy Deep Fried Leeks And A Balsamic Dressing

SERVES 4

20 large scallops

2 tomatoes, diced

5 basil leaves, shredded

4 leeks, shredded

2 shallots, chopped

100ml (3¹/₂ fl. oz) olive oil

salt

selection salad leaves

100ml (3¹/₂ fl. oz) balsamic vinegar

20 asparagus spears

1 lemon, cut into wedges

Sear the scallops in a hot non-stick pan until golden brown in colour. Add the diced tomatoes and shredded basil.

Deep fry the leeks and shallot in olive oil at 150°C until golden brown. This will take a few seconds. Drain on kitchen paper and dust lightly with salt.

Dress the salad leaves with the balsamic vinegar and divide them among four plates. Place five scallops on each plate and add the asparagus, tomatoes and scallop juices. Place the fried leek on top of the salad and serve with lemon wedges.

Greg Robinson

Crabmeat Au Gratin

SERVES 4

1½ tbsp butter

1½ tbsp plain flour

freshly ground black pepper

½ tsp salt

½ tsp paprika

570ml (1 pint) single cream

125g (4 oz) cheddar cheese, grated

1½ tbsp Worcestershire sauce

4 tbsp dry sherry or vermouth

450g (1lb) crabmeat (fresh if possible, but canned or frozen are ok)

75g (3oz) breadcrumbs

Melt the butter in a saucepan and stir in the flour, pepper, salt and paprika. Gradually blend in three-quarters of the cream, stirring constantly until the sauce is smooth. Add the grated cheese to the sauce with the Worcestershire sauce and stir until the cheese has melted. Gently fold in the crabmeat and sherry or vermouth. If the mixture appears too thick add a little of the remaining cream. The mixture should be soft enough to pile into 4 buttered scallop shells.

Sprinkle the crab-filled shells with the breadcrumbs and cook in a hot oven at 200°C/400°F/Gas Mark 6 for 15 to 20 minutes, or until the breadcrumbs are golden brown. Serve in the centre of a plate surrounded by buttered noodles and baby carrots.

Barbecued Swordfish With Green Mayonnaise

SERVES 4
4 x 200g (7 oz)
swordfish steaks

Marinade
1 tsp dried rosemary

1 clove garlic, finely
chopped

$1/2$ tsp cayenne

salt and pepper

Sauce
200ml (7 fl. oz)
mayonnaise

4 tbsp chopped
watercress

1 tbsp chopped
capers

1 tbsp chopped
gherkins

juice of $1/2$ lemon

salt and pepper

Mix all the marinade ingredients together. Place the fish in a shallow dish. Pour the marinade over and leave for 3 hours.

Meanwhile, blend the mayonnaise with the other ingredients and leave the flavours to develop.

Remove fish from the marinade and cook on a barbecue for about 4 minutes each side.

Serve with a little sauce on the side.

Mark Wogan

Smoked Haddock Fingers And Pommes Frites

SERVES 4

3 egg yolks

1 egg white

900g (2 lb) smoked haddock, cut into 6cm (2¹/₂ inch) fingers

seasoned flour

300g (10 oz) stale white breadcrumbs

oil, for frying

900g (2 lb) potatoes, peeled and cut into thin chips

Beat the egg yolks and white together. Coat the fish in flour, then egg, then breadcrumbs. Fry in the oil at 190°C/375°F for 8 minutes until golden brown.

Meanwhile, cook the frites in separate oil at 150°C/300°F for 5 to 7 minutes until tender but not coloured. Just before serving the fish, return the chips to the oil at 190°C/375°F and cook until golden brown. Serve in newspaper cones with salt and vinegar.

Aaron Patterson

Nage Of Seafood

SERVES 4

4 scallops

2 small fillets of red mullet/snapper

8 mussels or clams

2 small fillets of plaice or turbot

8 large prawns

a selection of young spring vegetables (about 675g/1½ lb)

Stock

1 small carrot

1 stick celery

1 shallot

1 clove garlic

150ml (¼ pint) water

150ml (¼ pint) dry white wine

thyme

chervil

tarragon

Prepare the fish by scrubbing shells, removing bones and checking clams and mussels are closed. To make the stock, cut the vegetables into small chunks and cover with the water. Bring to the boil and add the wine and herbs and allow to cool. Strain off the liquid and reserve.

Steam or simmer the spring vegetables until just tender. Use the stock to poach the fish starting with the biggest pieces. They should only need 5–7 minutes. Take care not to over cook the fish and shellfish. Check the mussels and clams are open and remove the black valve from the clams. Add the cooked vegetables and serve in a large bowl.

Paul Heathcote

Deep Fried Squid In Cracker Crumbs With Anchovy Mayonnaise

SERVES 4

900g (2 lb) squid, cleaned (ask the fishmonger to do this or buy ready cleaned and sliced at the supermarket)

2 eggs

5 anchovy fillets

juice of ¹/₂ lemon

25g (1oz) chopped parsley

150ml (¹/₄ pint) olive oil

pinch of cayenne pepper

Coating

125g (4 oz) plain flour

4 cream crackers, broken into crumbs and passed through a sieve

salt

150ml (¹/₄ pint) milk

Slice the squid into rings and any tentacles into short strips. In a food processor, combine eggs, anchovies, lemon juice and parsley. Slowly blend in the oil, drizzling it in drop by drop through the lid, to make the mayonnaise. Season with cayenne pepper.

Mix the flour and cracker crumbs together season with salt. Dip the squid into the milk and then roll in the flour and cracker mix. Fry at 180°C/350°F until golden brown. Serve with the anchovy mayonnaise.

Amanda Grant

Chermoula Fish With Marinated Courgette Strips

SERVES 4

4 large fillets sea bass

7 ripe tomatoes, quartered

3 green peppers, skinned and sliced

Chermoula
1 large onion, peeled and finely chopped

3 cloves garlic, peeled and finely chopped

1/2 tsp ground cumin

1/2 tsp paprika

1/2 tsp cayenne

1/2 tsp powdered saffron

6 tbsp fresh coriander, roughly chopped

4 tbsp parsley, roughly chopped

3 tbsp olive oil

juice of 1/2 lemon

pinch of salt

Courgette Strips
2 tbsp olive oil

1/2 tsp cayenne pepper

1/2 tsp cumin

600g courgettes

sea salt

freshly ground black pepper

2 lemons, halved, to serve

Combine all of the ingredients for the chermoula in a bowl and mix together well. Place the fish in a large dish and pour the chermoula over, cover and leave to marinate for at least 2 hours, or overnight.

Preheat the oven to 180°C/350°F/Gas Mark 4. Put the tomatoes and peppers into an ovenproof dish and place the fish on top, leave any excess chermoula behind, cover fish loosely with foil. Bake for at least 20 minutes or until the fish flakes easily at the touch of a fork.

Three minutes before the fish is cooked, prepare the courgette strips. Heat 2 tbsp olive oil in a large frying pan, add the cayenne and cumin and sauté for at least 2 minutes before adding the courgette slices. Sauté for a further 3 to 4 minutes, season with sea salt flakes and freshly ground black pepper.

To serve, arrange the courgette strips on 4 warmed serving plates. Place the peppers and tomatoes on top, followed by a fish fillet. Give each person half a lemon to squeeze over their fish.

Tessa Bramley

Fish And Chips With Red Sauce

SERVES 4

4 thick pieces of cod
weighing about
150–175g (5–6 oz)
each

salt and freshly
ground black
pepper

3 tbsp olive oil

30g (1 oz) unsalted
butter

1 small celeriac
(peeled and cut
into finger sized
'chips' – allow 6
per portion)

1 tbsp caster sugar
(unrefined)

stir-fried vegetables,
to serve

sprig of sweet cicely
(optional)

Rhubarb Sauce

2 pieces (whole stars)
of star anise

150ml ('/4 pint) well-
flavoured fish stock

150ml ('/4 pint)
rhubarb purée
(stew forced
rhubarb with 1 tbsp
water and 2 tsp
caster sugar)

30–45g (1–1'/2 oz)
unsalted butter,
chilled

Heat a griddle and also a cast-iron frying pan.
Season prepared fish. Oil surface with a little of
the olive oil. Griddle until golden.

Heat butter and remaining oil in hot pan.
Season celeriac, dust with caster sugar. Toss in
hot fat to colour. Tip into a roasting tin and roast
for 8–10 minutes at 240°C/475°F/Gas Mark 9
until golden and cooked through.

Carefully remove fish and sit golden side up
in roasting tin. Roast in hot oven for about 4
minutes and then rest in warm place until sauce
is made.

For the Rhubarb Sauce, add star anise
broken into pieces to fish stock and reduce by
half. Add rhubarb and seasonings and simmer
together. Pass through a fine sieve into a clean
pan and whisk in chilled butter to thicken and
give a gloss to the sauce.

Remove celeriac chips from oven and drain.
Sit cooked fish on a bed of stir-fried vegetables.
Arrange celeriac chips around. Pour rhubarb sauce
around fish. A sprig of sweet cicely would finish it
off.

Fried Cod Steaks With Tomato Fondue

SERVES 4

4 x 200g (7 oz) cod steaks (skin on)

4 tbsp flour

a little olive oil

500g (18 oz) young spinach leaves

pinch of freshly grated nutmeg

seasoning

Fondue
1 onion, sliced

2 cloves garlic

500g (18 oz) tomatoes (quartered)

100ml (3¹/₂ fl. oz) white wine (for vegetable stock)

seasoning

fresh basil leaves

Coat the fish (skin side only) with flour. Heat the oil in a frying pan and fry the fish skin-side down to crisp the skin. Turn fish over and seal other side. Reserve and roast in the oven for 7 minutes at 230°C/450°F/Gas Mark 8.

Wilt the spinach in a hot frying pan with a little oil, add the nutmeg and season.

Sweat off the onion and garlic in a heavy saucepan and add the tomatoes and wine (or stock). Cook for 15 to 20 minutes, then blend in a food processor and pass through a sieve. Season and serve.

Arrange the dish with the fish on a bed of spinach and the sauce around. Finish with a little basil.

Steven Saunders

Chilli, Sea Bass Oriental With Chinese Rice Noodles

SERVES 4

6 red chillies

2.5-cm (1-inch) square of fresh root ginger

4 spring onions

4 x 200g (7 oz) fillets of sea bass (boned but with skin left on)

100ml (3¹/₂ fl. oz) light soy sauce

2 tsp honey

2 tsp rice vinegar

200g (7 oz) rice noodles

1 tbsp oyster sauce

125g (4 oz) unsalted peanuts

1 tsp curry powder

Shred and deseed the chilli, shred the ginger and spring onions. Steam the sea bass on a butter wrapper with half of the ginger, spring onion and chilli for 10 minutes.

Prepare the sauce by mixing the soy sauce with the honey and vinegar. Add the remainder of ginger, spring onion and chilli.

Blanch the rice noodles in boiling water with a little salt, refresh under cold water. Fry the noodles in a wok with the oyster sauce and crushed peanuts and add a little curry powder. Serve the steamed sea bass on a bed of the noodles with the shredded chilli and ginger etc and the sauce around.

Main Courses
Meat & Poultry

Greg Robinson

Chicken And Almonds In A Calvados Sauce With Apples

SERVES 4

4 chicken portions

flour with salt and pepper, for dusting

40g (1½ oz) butter

6 tbsp Calvados

4 tbsp chicken stock

250ml (8–9 fl. oz) double cream

30g (1oz) toasted flaked almonds

Apple Wedges
4 dessert apples

50g (2 oz) butter, melted

Dust the chicken pieces in seasoned flour and fry in butter, over a moderate heat, until golden brown. Turn the chicken pieces over occasionally to ensure an even colour. Sprinkle the chicken with half of the Calvados and the chicken stock. Cover the pan tightly and simmer for 30 minutes or until the chicken is tender. Remove the chicken and keep warm. Add the remaining Calvados to the pan, scraping up any brown bits from the bottom and stir in the cream. Stir until heated through but do not boil and then season to taste. Spoon the sauce over the chicken and serve with the toasted almonds and the apple wedges.

To make the apple wedges, cut the apples into thick wedges removing the cores but leaving the skins on. Melt the butter in a frying pan and cook the apples until hot and golden. Be careful when turning them in the pan not to break them up.

Greg Robinson

Chicken Primavera

SERVES 4

16 small new
   potatoes, scrubbed

8 small onions, peeled

4 medium carrots,
   peeled and cut into
   thick strips

1 large parsnip,
   peeled and cut into
   finger-length strips

2 medium leeks,
   washed and cut
   into 1-cm (^{1}/$_2$-inch)
   lengths

4 chicken pieces
   (thigh and
   drumstick or whole
   poussin)

a little melted butter,
   for brushing

425 ml (^{3}/$_4$ pint)
   chicken stock

115ml (4 fl. oz) dry
   white wine

juice of ^{1}/$_2$ lemon

3 cloves garlic, peeled
   and chopped

a few sprigs of dried
   oregano and thyme

fresh ground black
   pepper

175g (6 oz) fresh or
   frozen peas

2 tbsp fresh parsley,
   chopped

Mix the potatoes, onions, carrots, parsnips and leeks in a roasting tin. Brush the chicken with a little melted butter and lay the pieces on top of the vegetables. Pour the stock and wine over the chicken with the lemon juice, and sprinkle with the garlic. Press the herbs into the vegetables and grind some fresh black pepper all over the dish before cooking uncovered for 1 hour 15 minutes, until no pink juices flow from the chicken when pierced.

During the cooking, stir the vegetables around and baste the chicken with the pan juices. Add the peas for the last 10–15 minutes of cooking time. If the juices evaporate too quickly during cooking, add a little more stock to prevent it drying out. Put the vegetables and chicken on to a large serving plate and scatter with the chopped parsley.

Aaron Patterson

Baby Chicken In Salt Crust

SERVES 4

4 whole poussin

selection of
  vegetables (green
  beans, new
  potatoes, baby
  carrots, turnips)

beaten egg and milk,
  to glaze

rock salt, to sprinkle

Salt Crust
1 kg (2 lb 3 oz)
  strong flour

700g (1¹/₂ lb) salt

4 egg whites

250ml (9 fl.oz) water

Chicken Sauce
250ml (9 fl. oz) dry
  sherry

16 Morel mushrooms
  (optional –
  cultivated will do)

200ml (7 fl. oz)
  whipping cream

250ml (9 fl. oz)
  strong chicken
  stock

salt and freshly
  ground black
  pepper

juice of ¹/₂ lemon

1 sprig rosemary,
  chopped

For the Salt Crust, mix together the flour, salt, egg whites and water until a dough is formed.

In a hot pan seal off the chicken until golden brown. Roll out the pastry and wrap the birds to form a bird shape. Egg wash and sprinkle with rock salt. Bake in a hot oven for 45 minutes until the pastry is golden, 220°C/425°F/Gas Mark 7.

To make the sauce, bring to the boil the sherry and the mushrooms for 2 minutes. Add cream and stock and simmer to reduce until it coats the back of the spoon. Season with salt, pepper, lemon juice and chopped rosemary.

To serve crack open the pastry around the chicken and serve with a selection of vegetables and the sauce.

Aaron Patterson

Poached Breast Of Chicken With A Light Broth Of Vegetables And Herbs

SERVES 4

2 shallots, chopped

1 clove garlic, chopped

150ml ('/4 pint) dry sherry (Tio Pepe)

150ml ('/4 pint) chicken stock

4 whole chicken breasts (skinned and bone free)

225g (8 oz) fresh tagliatelle pasta

salt and freshly ground black pepper

1 lemon

selection of baby vegetables (pre-cooked in 300ml ('/2 pint) of stock)

1 egg yolk

rosemary

chervil

parsley

chives

Gently fry the shallots and garlic until translucent in a large saucepan. Add the sherry and bring to the boil. Reduce for 1 minute and add the chicken stock. Add the chicken breast and cook gently for 10–15 minutes.

Meanwhile, cook the pasta in boiling salted water and season with salt, pepper and lemon juice. Warm up the baby vegetables, strain and season. Put the pasta in the centre of a deep dish and scatter the vegetables around.

In a stainless steel bowl, whisk the egg yolk with a drop of boiling water, over a bain marie until thick and creamy. Fold this into the chicken cooking juices and season. Chop the herbs and add to taste. Place the chicken breast on top of the pasta and pour the sauce over. Serve.

Aaron Patterson

Spiced Chicken

SERVES 6

1 x 2kg (4¹/₂ lb) chicken, jointed (or you could use thighs/drumsticks)

2 tbsp olive oil

150g (2 oz) brown basmati rice

2 fresh chillies, deseeded and finely chopped

1 tbsp coriander seeds

¹/₂ tsp saffron stamens

2 small thin-skinned lemons

2 large red peppers

2 large onions

3 cloves garlic, chopped

300ml (¹/₂ pint) chicken stock

150ml (¹/₄ pint) dry white wine

50g (2oz) pitted green olives

salt and pepper

30g (1oz) fresh coriander

Sear the chicken pieces in a large flameproof casserole in a little oil. Remove and set aside. Wash the rice. In a small pan quickly fry the chillies and coriander seeds in hot oil. Crush the saffron in a pestle and mortar. Add the lemon juice.

Fry off all the vegetables in the casserole pan until coloured, adding a little more oil if needed. Add the rice and seared chicken pieces. Add the chicken stock, white wine, cooked spice mixture and saffron. Cover with a lid and bake at 200°C/400°F/Gas Mark 6. Cook for about 1 hour until rice is cooked and chicken is tender. Scatter with coriander leaves and serve.

Paul Heathcote

Chicken And Mascarpone

SERVES 4

30g (1oz) pinenuts

1 clove garlic, crushed

2 sprigs basil

2 sprigs thyme

10 pink peppercorns

zest of 1 lemon

50g (2 oz)
Mascarpone cheese

1 tsp rock salt

1 x 1.8kg (4 lb)
chicken

Red Wine
Risotto

2 shallots, finely diced

1 clove garlic, finely
chopped

50g (2 oz) button
mushrooms, sliced

50g (2 oz) butter

300g (10 oz) arborio
rice

1/2 bottle Valpolicella

1 1/2 litres (2 1/2 pints)
chicken stock
(approximately)

50g (2 oz) freshly
grated Parmesan
cheese

Toast the nuts under a grill until brown. Blend in a food processor with the garlic, herbs, peppercorns and lemon zest. Add the Mascarpone and salt last.

Prepare the chicken by removing the wishbone, loosen the skin from the breasts and place the cheese mix under the skin. Tie the chicken and roast for 1 1/2 hours at 180°C/350°F/Gas Mark 4 or until the juices run clear.

To make the risotto, gently fry the shallots, garlic and mushrooms in the butter, add the rice and cook without colouring until transparent. Add 1/2 the wine and cook until sticky. Add the remaining wine and repeat. Add the stock stage by stage, repeating the process as for wine. When the risotto is cooked, add the Parmesan cheese. Season with salt and pepper and serve with the chicken.

Marinated Chicken With Raisin And Almond Salad

SERVES 4

4 chicken breasts

Marinade

2 tbsp ground ginger

1 tsp cinnamon

1 onion, chopped

2 tsp ground almonds

2 tbsp olive oil

juice of ½ lemon

salt and pepper, to taste

a few strands of saffron

Salad

100g (3½ oz) raisins

100g (3½ oz) blanched whole almonds

2 plum tomatoes, chopped

100g (3½ oz) cooked chick peas

black olives

olive oil

Mix all the marinade ingredients together. Score the chicken well, making deep incisions. Season the chicken with salt and pepper and coat with the marinade. Leave for approximately 1 hour. Barbecue over hot coals or grill until cooked through and juices run clear, brushing with a little marinade after turning.

Combine all the salad ingredients, dressing with a little olive oil to taste. Serve the cooked chicken with the salad.

Steven Saunders

Chicken And Tomato Roulade With Madeira Cream

SERVES 4

4 chicken breasts
(boneless and
skinned)

8–12 leaves of
spinach

8 slices sun-dried
tomatoes

8 spears thin
asparagus

seasoning

chicken stock, for
poaching

sprig of chervil, to
garnish

Sauce

2 tbsp dry Madeira

4 tbsp chicken stock

100ml (3^1/$_2$ fl. oz)
double cream

seasoning

Place the chicken breast between 2 pieces of cling film and flatten slightly with a rolling pin. Blanch the spinach in boiling water until tender and refresh immediately. Lay spinach, tomato and asparagus pieces on to the chicken breast and season. Roll the chicken up in the cling film into a roulade and poach in boiling water and chicken stock (50/50) for approximately 15 minutes until cooked. Remove and allow to rest.

Meanwhile, reduce the Madeira and add 4 tbsp chicken stock. Now add the cream, reduce again and season. Taste.

Cut each chicken breast into 3 even-sized pieces and arrange on the plates with the sauce around.

Marinaded Butterflied Leg Of Lamb With Mustard Sauce

SERVES 4

1.4kg (3lb) leg of lamb (butterflied – ask your butcher to do this)

Marinade
1/2 medium onion, chopped

2.5-cm (1-inch) cube of fresh ginger, chopped

1 tbsp coriander seeds (dry toasted for 5 minutes and crushed)

3 cloves garlic, halved

1 tbsp black peppercorns, crushed

2 tbsp sea salt

8 tbsp lemon juice

4 tbsp olive oil

small handful fresh coriander leaves, chopped

Sauce
3 large ripe tomatoes, cored and roughly chopped

250ml (9 fl.oz) dry white wine

3 tbsp Dijon mustard

125g (4oz) lightly salted butter, in small pieces

salt and black pepper

Place all the ingredients for the marinade in a bowl and mix together. Place the lamb in a glass dish and spread the marinade all over it. Cover the dish and marinate the lamb in the fridge for 2 days, turning once or twice during that time.

To cook, drain the lamb and reserve the marinade. Heat the grill or barbecue until hot. Wipe the lamb dry and place under the heat (or over it) and cook for 10 minutes, basting with some of the marinade. Turn the lamb over and cook for a further 10 minutes or longer if you prefer it not pink. Brush the cooked lamb with any remaining marinade and leave for 5 minutes before slicing.

To make the sauce, bring the tomatoes and wine to the boil. Lower the heat and simmer for about 20 minutes, or until the mixture is thick. Press the mixture, plus 4 tbsp of the reserved marinade through a fine sieve into a heatproof bowl. Beat the mustard into the mixture and then set the bowl over a pan of simmering water. Beat in the butter a little at a time until fully incorporated. Season to taste. Serve with the lamb.

Greg Robinson

Spicy Lamb

SERVES 4

2–3 tbsp oil

900g (2lb) lamb, cubed into 2.5-cm (1-inch) pieces

2 onions, chopped

2 cloves garlic, chopped

2 red chillies, deseeded and chopped large

2 tbsp curry powder (strength to taste)

2 tbsp tomato purée

300ml ($\frac{1}{2}$ pint) coconut milk

300ml ($\frac{1}{2}$ pint) lamb stock

1 fresh bay leaf

$\frac{1}{2}$ tsp ground allspice

salt and pepper

225g (8 oz) carrots, sliced

225g (8 oz) pineapple, chopped

2 tbsp lime juice

rice and West Indian bread, to serve

Heat the oil in a frying pan and fry the lamb pieces until brown. Remove the lamb to a casserole. Using the same frying pan, fry the onion, garlic and chillies until the onions are browned. Add the curry powder and tomato purée and cook for a further 2–3 minutes. Add the coconut milk and stock to the pan and stir to pick up any bits from the bottom of the pan. Pour the onion mixture on to the lamb and add the bay leaf, allspice and seasoning to taste. Reduce the heat and simmer for 1$\frac{1}{2}$ hours.

Add the sliced carrots and continue cooking for 30 minutes or until the meat and carrots are tender. Finally, add the pineapple and lime juice cook for a further 5 minutes before serving with rice and West Indian flat bread.

Saddle Of West Country Lamb

SERVES 6

2.3kg (5 lb) saddle of lamb (removed from the bone, then re-tied)

2 cloves garlic, slivered

some rosemary sprigs

2 tsp flour

400ml (14 fl. oz) lamb stock

2 tbsp redcurrant jelly

4 parsnips, peeled and cut into disks

5 carrots, peeled and cut into disks

4 red peppers, deseeded and cut into quarters

1 medium onion, peeled and sliced

a few sprigs of fresh thyme

6 cloves of garlic (unpeeled)

125ml (4 fl. oz) olive oil

salt and freshly ground black pepper

Make incisions in the skin of the lamb and insert slivers of garlic and a sprig of rosemary. Repeat until the flesh is covered. Preheat the oven to 200°C/400°F/Gas Mark 6 and roast the lamb for 1^1/$_2$ hours until pink.

Place the vegetables altogether in a large roasting tray with the unpeeled garlic and thyme. Pour over the olive oil and season with salt and pepper. Place in the same oven as the meat for 1 hour.

Remove the lamb from the oven and place on a carving tray. Place the lamb roasting tray on the hob over a medium heat, add the flour and cook for 2 minutes. Slowly add the stock, then bring to the boil. Sieve into a pan and add the redcurrant jelly and heat until dissolved.

Remove the string from the lamb and slice the loin into medallions. Serve with the sauce on a bed of the roasted vegetables.

Mark Wogan

Marinated Butterfly Lamb With Roast New Potatoes

SERVES 4

1.1kg (2¹/₂ lb) leg of lamb (boneless weight – ask your butcher to bone and flatten or 'butterfly' it for you)

150ml (¹/₄ pint) dry sherry

150ml (¹/₄ pint) port

3 tbsp soy sauce

4 tbsp honey

2 tbsp tomato purée

4 tbsp fresh herbs (rosemary, oregano, parsley, mint)

900g (2 lb) new potatoes

8 cloves garlic

sprigs of fresh thyme

5 tbsp olive oil

rock salt

Place the meat in a large strong clean plastic bag. In a bowl, mix the sherry, port, soy, honey, tomato purée and herbs until combined. Pour into the bag, seal and refrigerate overnight. Place the potatoes in a disposable tin-foil tray. Throw in the garlic, thyme and pour over oil. Sprinkle with the rock salt. Seal the tray with foil. Cook on the barbecue for 25 minutes, shaking to turn occasionally.

Remove meat from bag and discard the bag. Place the meat skin side down on the barbeque for 10 minutes, then turn and cook for a further 30–35 minutes with the lid of the barbeque down or with a dome of tin foil over the lamb. Serve on a large platter sliced and surrounded by the potatoes.

Aaron Patterson

Chump Of Lamb With Roasted Mediterranean Vegetables

SERVES 4

1 chump of lamb
(about 1kg/2¹/₄ lb)

olive oil

30g (1oz) butter

¹/₂ red pepper

¹/₂ yellow pepper

1 tbsp balsamic
vinegar

1 slice aubergine

2 tsp tapenade (Greek
black olive purée)

3 cherry tomatoes

1 sprig rosemary

3 cloves garlic, peeled

4 tbsp lamb stock

500g (18 oz)
courgettes

1 tbsp tomato purée

Fry the lamb until golden brown in a little oil and butter.

Peel and deseed the peppers, and soften in a little olive oil. Deglaze the pan with balsamic vinegar. Fry the aubergine until still firm.

Lay out a piece of silver foil. Place the lamb in the middle with 1 tsp tapenade spread on top. Lay the peppers, aubergine and tomatoes around. Add a little chopped rosemary, 1 clove chopped garlic, lamb stock and a little oil. Seal up the parcel and bake in a hot oven 220°C/425°F/ Gas Mark 7 for 10–15 minutes.

Thickly slice the courgettes and place in a roasting pan with the remaining garlic. Drizzle well with olive oil. Roast until tender and starting to char.

Pour all the juices from the lamb foil into a pan and add 1 teaspoon of tapenade, a little chopped rosemary and the tomato purée.

Remove the lamb and allow to rest for a further 5 minutes before serving with the garlic roasted courgettes and the sauce.

Aaron Patterson

Salad Of Lamb

SERVES 4
1 small aubergine
2 small courgettes
150ml (¹/₄ pint) olive oil
salt and pepper
125g (4 oz) French beans
2 tomatoes
4 small lamb fillets
mixed salad leaves

Dressing
1 tbsp balsamic vinegar
3 tbsp olive oil
rosemary sprigs, to garnish

Dice the aubergine and courgettes. Pan fry the aubergine in about 3 tbsp hot olive oil for 1 minute and add the courgettes. Season with salt and pepper.

Blanch the beans in boiling salted water for 3 minutes. Blanch the tomatoes in boiling water for 10 seconds and refresh. Peel off the skins, and de-seed, finely chop. Mix all the vegetables together in a dish.

Preheat the oven to 230°C/450°F/ Gas Mark 8. Sear the lamb in the remaining olive oil and roast in the oven for approximately 5 minutes. Allow to rest for 3 minutes.

To make the dressing: pour into a bowl 1 tbsp of cooking juices from the lamb and add the vinegar, oil and seasoning. Whisk together.

Slice the lamb thinly and season. Dress the vegetables and salad leaves and place in the middle of a plate. Place the lamb around the salad and serve.

Loin Of Lamb And Mediterranean Vegetables

SERVES 4

2 red peppers, deseeded and sliced

2 yellow peppers, deseeded and sliced

2 shallots, peeled and sliced

2 courgettes, peeled and sliced

1 aubergine, peeled and sliced

3 cloves garlic

4 tbsp olive oil

30g (1 oz) chopped basil and rosemary

2 tbsp tomato purée

salt and pepper

4 x 150g (2 oz) small loins of lamb, boned and trimmed

1 tsp garlic purée

a few sprigs thyme

1 jar Greek black olive tapenade

30g (1oz) butter

new potatoes

Fry the peppers, shallot, courgette, aubergine and 3 cloves garlic in 3 tablespoons of the olive oil separately until soft. Add the basil and half of the tomato purée. Season. Place the mixture in a metal ring, patting it down so it will hold together when the ring is removed.

Fry the lamb in olive oil until brown. Add garlic purée and some thyme.

Roast in a hot oven for 8 minutes. Allow to rest for a further 3–4 minutes.

Add half a tablespoon of water to the frying pan along with the tapenade, remaining tomato purée and the chopped rosemary and basil. Add lamb juices, thicken with butter and season.

Place vegetables on plate (remove ring). Slice the lamb in $1/2$ lengthways and place on plate. Spoon sauce to one side. Serve with minted new potatoes.

Paul Heathcote

Roast Lamb With Raisins And Couscous

SERVES 4

1.4kb (1 lb) leg of lamb, boned

salt and pepper

2 sprigs thyme

2 sprigs rosemary

1 clove garlic, crushed

50g (2 oz) raisins

2 tsp grated lemon zest

2 tbsp olive oil

1 tsp balsamic vinegar

30g (1 oz) breadcrumbs

Cous Cous

1/2 onion, finely diced

1 clove garlic, crushed

30g (1 oz) cashew nuts

1/2 green pepper, diced

30g (1 oz) mushrooms, sliced

30g (1 oz) butter

olive oil

225g (8 oz) couscous

4 mint leaves, chopped

Prepare the leg of lamb by removing some of the gristle and fat. Criss cross the inside with a sharp knife. Season with salt, pepper, herbs and garlic.

Place the raisins in a pan with a little water and the lemon zest and boil until plump. Drain and chop. Add the oil, vinegar, breadcrumbs and mix together. Spread the raisin mixture inside the leg and tie. Cook at 180°C/350°F/Gas Mark 4 for about 1 hour 15 minutes. Allow to rest before carving.

To make the couscous, gently fry the onion, garlic, nuts, pepper and mushrooms in the butter and a little oil.

Pour 30ml (12 fl. oz) boiling water over the couscous and allow to stand. After 3 minutes all the water should be absorbed. Stir in the onion mixture from the frying pan. Season with salt and pepper and mint and serve with the lamb.

Lamb D'azure Served With Mint Mash

SERVES 4

4 lamb shanks (approximately 250g (9 oz) each)

6 tbsp olive oil

5 cloves garlic, peeled and halved

1 tbsp fresh thyme

2 tbsp fresh oregano

salt and freshly ground black pepper

2 aubergines

2 large onions, peeled and sliced

450g (1 lb) fresh plum tomatoes, skinned and cut in half

2 tbsp tomato purée

100g (3¹/₂ oz) black olives

100g (3¹/₂ oz) green olives

200ml (7fl. oz) red wine

fresh thyme and oregano to garnish

Mint Mash

175g (6oz) freshly chopped mint

50g (2 oz) butter

900g (2 lb) mashed potatoes

4 tbsp milk

Preheat the oven to 180°C/350°F/Gas Mark 4. Put the lamb shanks into a large bowl, cover with 4 tbsp olive oil, garlic, thyme and oregano and season well with salt and pepper. Leave to marinate at room temperature while you prepare the vegetables.

Cut the aubergine into chunks and place in a colander, sprinkle with salt, place a plate on top and weight it down with tins of food to remove bitter juices, leave for 30 minutes. Heat the remaining 2 tbsp of olive oil in large frying pan, sauté the onion slices until brown. Put into a large roasting tin.

Scrape the marinade off the lamb. Brown the lamb in the frying pan on all sides and put into the roasting tin with the remaining marinade. Cook in the preheated oven for 25 minutes.

Remove the meat from the oven and pour away any excess fat. Add the aubergines, tomatoes, tomato purée and olives. Pour in the wine, mix together well and season with freshly ground black pepper and salt. Return the meat to the pan and return to the oven for a further 1¹/₂ hours or until the lamb is tender. Spoon off excess fat.

To make the Mint Mash, mix the mint, butter and mashed potatoes together, adding milk to the desired consistency.

Spoon the mint mash on to warm serving plates and divide the lamb and vegetables among them, arranging them on top. Garnish with fresh herbs.

Steven Saunders

Lamb Fillets Provençale

SERVES 4

4 lamb fillets

150ml ('/4 pint) olive oil

3 cloves garlic, crushed

1 sprig fresh rosemary, chopped

1 red pepper, deseeded and chopped into small dice

1 green pepper, deseeded and chopped into small dice

1 aubergine, chopped into small dice

2 courgettes, chopped into small dice

200ml (7 fl. oz) lamb stock (with Madeira)

100ml (3¹/₂ fl. oz) red wine

1 sprig fresh mint or chervil

Rosti

900g (2 lb) potatoes, grated

1 tsp paprika pepper

salt

vegetable oil, for frying

Put the lamb fillets into a marinade made from 100ml (3¹/₂ fl. oz) olive oil, garlic and rosemary. Leave for 8 hours or overnight.

In 3 separate hot frying pans, sweat off the peppers, aubergine and courgettes in a little oil.

Prepare rosti by squeezing out grated potato in a cloth. Season with paprika and salt, and fry in vegetable oil in a hot pan inside 10-cm (4-inch) rings until golden and crisp.

Remove lamb from the marinade and griddle on a hot griddle pan for 3 minutes. Season well. Heat the lamb stock with the red wine and reduce slightly. Season. Turn over lamb and griddle other side for 2–3 minutes. Leave to rest away from heat. Slice lamb thinly and arrange on each rosti.

Mix the vegetables together to form a ratatouille and place a few in the middle of each rosti. Scatter the remainder of ratatouille around each lamb rosti and serve the sauce over. Garnish with a sprig of fresh mint or chervil.

BBQ Rib Of Beef With Garlic, Yoghurt And Cumin

SERVES 4

1 rib of beef
(approximately
1.5kg/3 lb)

4 cloves garlic

100ml (3^1/$_2$ fl. oz)
natural yoghurt

1 tsp ground cumin

^{1}/$_2$ lemon, juice and
rind

2 sprigs thyme,
chopped

1 red chilli (chopped)

rock salt

crushed black
peppercorns

Ask your butcher to prepare the rib of beef by hand, sawing between the rib bone, effectively making two cutlets. Trim off some of the excess fat and nick the outside of the rib fat so that it does not curl up on cooking. Cut garlic cloves in half and with the point of a sharp knife, make a few incisions in the fat side and push the garlic cloves inside.

Combine yoghurt, cumin, lemon rind, thyme and chilli together with the salt and peppercorns. Pour the lemon juice over the ribs, followed by the yoghurt mixture and leave for 2 hours. Scrape off the yoghurt mix, allowing some to remain and barbecue until the beef is cooked to your taste. Serve with caramelised fried onions.

Aaron Patterson

Classic Roast Pork with Crackling And Cider Fondant Potatoes And Roasted Apples

SERVES 4

1.5kg (3 lb) loin of pork (on the bone, wide rib end)

2 large potatoes

125g (4 oz) butter

150ml (¼ pint) cider

2 large apples

75g (3 oz) icing sugar

oil, for frying

carrots, red cabbage, baby turnips, and gravy, to serve

Score the rind of the pork and rub in salt. Leave for 24 hours. This will help it to crisp while cooking.

Peel the potatoes and cut in half. Place into a thick-bottomed ovenproof pan with the butter and the cider. Cook until golden brown.

Peel and core the apples and cut in half. Dip one side in the icing sugar. Caramelise in a hot non stick pan with a little oil.

Roast the pork in a roasting pan on a high shelf in the oven at 220°C/425°F/Gas Mark 7 for 25 minutes. Reduce the heat to 190°C/375°F/Gas Mark 5 and cook for a further 1–1½ hours. To tell if the meat is cooked, insert a skewer into the thickest part of the pork. The juices that run out should be absolutely clear, without any trace of pinkness. Take the pork out of the oven and leave to rest for 15 minutes. Serve with seasonal vegetables, fondant potatoes, roasted apples and gravy.

Calves Liver With Pancetta And Caramelised Onions

SERVES 4

4 x 110g slices calves liver (approximately 125g/4 oz each)

vegetable oil

250ml (9 fl. oz) veal jus

¹/₂ bottle Madeira

2 onions, thinly sliced

¹/₂ bottle red wine

1 tbsp white wine vinegar

1 tbsp caster sugar

4 portions crushed (not mashed) potatoes

100ml (3¹/₂ fl. oz) double cream

2 cloves garlic

8 slices pancetta

seasoning

chervil, to garnish

Slice the liver thinly and place in vegetable oil to cover. Heat a griddle.

Reduce the veal jus and Madeira by half. Sweat the onions with the red wine, vinegar and sugar and cook until translucent. Heat the potatoes and boil the cream and garlic together and add to the potatoes.

Griddle the liver for 15–20 seconds each side and reserve. Griddle the pancetta until golden and crisp.

Serve the liver on a ring of curled potatoes with the onions on top and two pieces of pancetta. Season the sauce and spoon around. Garnish with chervil.

Main Courses
Vegetarian

Mark Wogan

Individual Spinach Tarts With Red Pesto Sauce

SERVES 4

400g (14 oz) short crust pastry (made-weight)

500g (18 oz) cooked spinach

4 eggs

200g (7 oz) fresh ricotta

50g (2 oz) freshly grated parmesan

pinch of nutmeg

salt and pepper

100g (3¹/₂ oz) red pesto sauce

4 tbsp mayonnaise

4 tbsp water

salad leaves, to serve

Roll out the pastry, line four individual loose-bottomed flan rings and refrigerate for 20 minutes. Preheat the oven to 200°C/400°F/Gas Mark 6 and bake the pastry cases blind for 10 minutes.

Meanwhile, chop the spinach. Beat the eggs and cheese together and add the spinach. Season with the nutmeg, salt and pepper. Pour the mixture into the partly-cooked pastry cases and bake for 25 minutes. The flans should be golden on top and set.

Make the sauce by blending together the pesto, mayonnaise, and water until a pouring consistency is achieved. Serve the tarts with a little of the sauce and some fresh salad leaves.

Sweet Potato And Chestnut Cakes

SERVES 4

450g (1 lb) purple-skinned sweet potatoes

225g (8 oz) canned chestnuts

75g (3 oz) butter

salt and pepper

1/2 tsp ground mace

2 tbsp chopped parsley

1 large Spanish onion

300g (10 oz) cherry tomatoes

5 tbsp olive oil

1 tbsp brown sugar

flour for coating

1 egg, beaten

125g (4 oz) stale breadcrumbs

Peel and cut the potatoes and steam for 20 minutes. Place in a bowl with the chestnuts and mash with the butter until smooth. Season with the salt and pepper and mace and add the parsley. Make the mixture into eight balls and refrigerate.

Meanwhile, preheat the oven to its highest setting, slice the onion thinly and place in an oven-proof dish with the cherry tomatoes and olive oil and sprinkle with brown sugar. Season and place uncovered in the oven for 30 minutes.

Season the flour and roll the cakes in the flour, then in the egg and then in the breadcrumbs. Chill again for 10 minutes. Heat 1cm (1/2 inch) deep of oil, on a medium heat and fry the cakes in batches until golden on both sides.

Serve 2 cakes per person on a bed of the warm tomato salad.

Mark Wogan

Herby Soufflé Omelette

SERVES 4

4 eggs, separated

2 tbsp mixed fresh chopped herbs (parsley/basil/thyme)

50g (2 oz) fresh grated Parmesan

50g (2 oz) air-cured ham, chopped

salt and pepper

knob of butter

Beat the yolks together with the herbs, Parmesan and ham. Season. Beat the whites until stiff then combine gently folding with the yolk mix.

Heat the butter in a large frying pan. When just foaming; pour in the eggs and cook for 3 minutes over a medium heat, then place under a medium grill until golden brown and risen. Score down the middle of the omelette. Fold in half and serve with a herb salad.

Aaron Patterson

Tartlet Of Vegetables

SERVES 4

1 thin pastry case 25cm (10 inches) across, baked

1 yellow pepper

1 red pepper

1 courgette

1 clove garlic, crushed

1/2 tsp rosemary

1/2 aubergine, sliced

15g (1/2 oz) butter

15g (1/2 oz) brown sugar

4 halves sun-dried tomatoes

2 tbsp tapenade

6 tbsp balsamic vinegar

100g (3 1/2 oz) Mozzarella cheese

Place the pastry case on a baking sheet. Blanch the peppers or hold over a flame or under the grill until the skins peel away easily. Cut into quarters, discarding the stalks and seeds. Cook the flesh in a hot pan until soft. Slice the courgette and fry in the olive oil with the garlic and rosemary until softened. Fry the aubergine slices in a shallow pan in the butter and sugar. Turn them until softened and well glazed. Warm all the vegetables in the vinegar.

Spread the tapenade on the bottom of the pastry case, and place the warm vegetables on the top.

Put a few slices of Mozzarella on the top and grill until soft.

Desserts

Greg Robinson

Chocolate Almond Layer Cake

SERVES 8

350g (12 oz) marzipan

150ml (¹/₄ pint) sour cream

250g (9 oz) dark chocolate (good quality)

150g (5 oz) butter

75g (3 oz) golden caster sugar

5 eggs, separated

125g (4 oz) plain flour

125g (4 oz) cornflour

2 tbsp Amaretto

150ml (¹/₄ pint) double cream

Grease and base line a 20-cm (8-inch) round loose-bottomed or spring-sided cake tin.

Chop the marzipan and place in a saucepan with the sour cream, 100g (3¹/₂ oz) of the chocolate (chopped and grated) and the butter. Heat gently until the mixture is melted and smooth. Remove the pan from the heat and beat in the sugar, egg yolks, flours and liqueur.

Whisk the egg whites until stiff and fold carefully into the mixture. Spread about 4 tbsp of the mixture evenly over the bottom of the tin and place under a preheated hot grill, until the mixture is browned and firm to the touch. Repeat this process until all the mixture is used up. This should make between 15–20 layers.

Allow to cool in the tin. Carefully remove the cake from the tin and remove the base paper. Put the remaining chocolate and the double cream into a bowl over a pan of simmering water. Stir until smooth, and then allow to cool until thick enough to spread over the cake in a swirling pattern.

Greg Robinson

Chocolate Yoghurt Scones With Strawberries And Clotted Cream

MAKES ABOUT 8

225g (8 oz) self-raising flour

2 tsp baking powder

50g (2 oz) butter

30g (1 oz) caster sugar

3 tbsp cocoa powder

150g (5 oz) pot natural yoghurt

clotted or thick double cream

good quality strawberry jam

icing sugar, to dust

strawberries

chocolate sauce

Sieve the flour and baking powder into a bowl. Cut the butter into small pieces and rub into the flour. Add the sugar and sieved cocoa powder and mix thoroughly.

Empty the yoghurt into the mixture and stir to mix in completely. If the mixture is too sticky to handle, add a little more flour. Knead the mixture softly until there are no cracks and then quickly roll out to a thickness of 2cm (³/₄ inch).

Cut out rounds using a 6-cm (2¹/₂-inch) pastry cutter, and bake on a greased tray in a hot oven set at 220°C/425°F/Gas Mark 7 for about 10 minutes – or until well risen.

Cool on a wire rack. To serve, cut in half and spread generously with clotted cream. Add a spoonful of good quality strawberry jam and top with the other half of the scone. Sprinkle with a dusting of icing sugar and place a whole strawberry on top of the scone. Add an extra spoonful of clotted cream and drizzle with chocolate sauce.

Chocolate And Tia Maria Soufflé With Mocha Ice Cream

SERVES 4

225g (8 oz) bitter dark chocolate

4 tsp Tia Maria

5 egg whites, chilled

pinch of salt

4 tbsp caster sugar

icing sugar, to dust

mocha ice cream, to serve

Melt the chocolate gently in a double boiler or in a bowl over a pan of hot water (taking care that no water or steam gets into the chocolate) and stir the chocolate gently.

Preheat oven to 240°C/475°F/Gas Mark 9. Lightly grease and sugar 4 small pretty ramekins.

Remove chocolate from heat source and allow to cool a little. It must still be liquid. Pour 1 tbsp of chocolate and 1 tsp of Tia Maria into each ramekin.

Whisk chilled egg whites with the salt until stiff. Add 1 tsp sugar and whisk until glossy stiff peaks. Add half the sugar and whisk back to stiff peaks. Repeat with remaining sugar.

Working gently and quickly, fold the chocolate into whites using a balloon whisk to fold it in. Pour into the 4 ramekins and put into the hot oven immediately for 5 minutes until well risen and crusty on top. As soon as the soufflés are cooked, dust lightly with icing sugar and serve immediately with a scoop of Mocha Ice Cream.

The resultant soufflé has a crusty top, a dreamy light middle and a liquid centre.

Tessa Bramley

Wicked Chocolate Shortbread Tart

SERVES 6

Shortbread
Pastry

50g (2 oz) unsalted butter

50g (2 oz) caster sugar

75g (3 oz) plain flour

30g (1 oz) semolina

Wicked
Chocolate
Filling

175g (6 oz) dark bitter chocolate (with a high cocoa butter content)

6 tbsp brandy

3 tbsp cornflour (rounded measure)

400g (14 oz) caster sugar

4 size 2 eggs, beaten

600ml (1 pint) single cream

1 split vanilla pod

200g (7 oz) unsalted butter

chocolate curls or leaves, to decorate

Cream the butter with the sugar and work in the flour and semolina to a soft dough. Chill for at least an hour. Press into a 20-cm (8-inch) flan tin and smooth the base and up the sides. Line with crumpled greaseproof paper and baking beans. Bake blind at 200°C/400°F/Gas Mark 6 for 10 minutes. Remove the paper and beans and return to the oven for 5–10 minutes to crisp and colour. Allow to become cold.

Melt chocolate and brandy in a double boiler or in a basin over a pan of hot water. Blend cornflour, sugar and beaten eggs with a little of the cream. Heat the rest of the cream with the vanilla pod and then stir into the blended egg mixture. Cook gently, stirring all the time until mixture thickens and the cornflour is cooked out – taste it but do not boil. This will take about 6–8 minutes. Remove vanilla pod. Cool slightly and then beat in melted butter.

Pour into the cold shortbread tart case and leave to set. The tart will have a high gloss on the surface and needs little embellishment. Decorate with chocolate curls or a cluster of chocolate leaves.

Lemon And Chocolate Cheesecake With Chocolate And Walnut Base

SERVES 8

Base
300g (10 oz) dark
 chocolate digestive
 biscuits, crumbled

75g (3 oz) finely
 chopped walnuts

100g (3¹/₂ oz) butter

30g (1 oz) bitter dark
 chocolate, for curls

Filling
425g (15 oz)
 Mascarpone

2 lemons

¹/₂ tsp natural vanilla
 essence

3 eggs (size 2)

200g (7 oz) caster
 sugar

Topping
150ml (¹/₄ pint) sour
 cream

nutmeg

Stir the biscuits, nuts and butter in a pan until the butter is melted and they are mixed together. Press into the base of a greased 25-cm (10-inch) flan tin. Chill in the freezer.

In a large bowl, whisk together the cheese, zest from 2 lemons and juice from 1¹/₂ and vanilla essence until it forms a soft smooth floppy mixture. Using the mixer, whisk the eggs and sugar together until they form a thick trail which will stay on the surface. Gently mix the egg mixture into the cheese mixture (i.e. light into heavy) using a balloon whisk or spatula.

Stand the tin on a baking sheet. Pour filling on to the cheesecake base, filling the tin right to the top. Bake at 140°C/275°F/Gas Mark 1 for 30 minutes.

While still warm, pour over the sour cream. The sour cream will set to a smooth, glossy finish. Grate a little nutmeg on top, and finish with some chocolate curls.

Tessa Bramley

Bitter Chocolate Teardrops Of Strawberry And White Chocolate Mousse

SERVES 8

Teardrops

50g (2 oz) bitter chocolate, melted and poured into 2 greaseproof piping bags

8 strips acetate (cut approximately 5 x 30cm/2 x 12 inch – the sort used for model making)

Mousse

1 leaf gelatine

150ml (^{1}/$_4$ pint) thick strawberry purée

1 tbsp strawberry liqueur

125g (4 oz) white chocolate

50g (2 oz) caster sugar

2 tbsp water

3 egg whites (size 2)

450ml (16 fl. oz) double cream, lightly whipped and chilled

strawberry or chocolate sauce and whole strawberries, to decorate

Put the gelatine in a bowl and cover with cold water. Warm the purée and liqueur, squeeze out the softened gelatine and add to the purée. Stir to dissolve. Set on one side to cool and start setting.

Melt chocolate gently in a double boiler and then cool.

In a heavy-based pan, dissolve the sugar and water. Bring to the boil and then simmer until a 'large ball' stage is reached (use a sugar thermometer 121–124°C/250–255°F). In an electric mixer, whisk the egg whites to stiff peaks and then keeping the mixer running, pour the sugar slowly down the side of the bowl – whisking until the meringue is cold – about 2 minutes (Italian Meringue).

Fold the melted chocolate into the cooled meringue, then the strawberry concentrate and then the cream. Fill a piping bag and chill until ready to use.

Cut off the ends of the greaseproof bags containing the chocolate and pipe squiggles of bitter chocolate over the acetate to form a rough lattice effect. Pick up the two ends of the acetate and stick together chocolate side inwards to form a large teardrop shape. Chill in the fridge until ready to serve. Carefully peel away the acetate leaving a chocolate shape. Place a shape in each serving plate and fill with chocolate strawberry mousse. Pour a little strawberry sauce or chocolate sauce onto the plate and garnish with a few strawberries.

Hot Chocolate Soufflé With Pistachio Ice Cream

SERVES 4

150ml (¼ pint) water

250g (9 oz) cocoa powder, mixed to a smooth paste with a little water

8 egg whites

4 tbsp caster sugar

50g (2 oz) chopped chocolate

4 scoops ice cream (pistachio or vanilla)

melted butter and sugar, for pots

Lightly brush 4 individual soufflé pots with melted butter and allow to set slightly. Line with sugar.

Bring the water to the boil and add to the cocoa powder paste until smooth.

Whisk the egg whites and gradually add the sugar until soft peaks are formed. Fold in ½ of the egg whites to the cocoa mix. Add the remainder, being careful to mix thoroughly without knocking too much of the air out.

Fill the soufflé pots halfway and then place some of the chopped chocolate in the centre. Top with more soufflé mix and level off at the top. Place in a preheated oven – 200°C/400°F/Gas Mark 6 for 10 to 12 minutes. Serve with pistacho or vanilla ice cream.

Jean Davies

Chocolate Pastry Fruit Tart

SERVES 4

6 fresh figs, washed and dried

3 kiwi fruit, skinned and sliced

1 papaya

175g (6 oz) apple jelly, for glaze

Chocolate Pastry
125g (4 oz) unbleached plain flour

1 1/2 tbsp cocoa

1 1/2 tbsp sugar

100g (3 1/2 oz) unsalted butter

50g (2 oz) vegetarian lard

5 tbsp cold water

Marshmallow Custard
175g (6 oz) dark chocolate

100g (3 1/2 oz) marshmallows

50g (2 oz) roasted almonds, finely chopped

2 tbsp sherry

200ml (7 fl. oz) double cream

For the pastry, sift the flour, cocoa and sugar together in a blender. Cut the butter into small pieces and add to the flour mixture with the lard and blend until the mixture looks like breadcrumbs. Add the cold water and mix until the pastry begins to form a ball. Form the pastry into 2 equal flat circles. Wrap and refrigerate for 30 minutes.

Melt the chocolate and marshmallows in a basin over a pan of gently steaming water. Remove from the heat and leave to cool. When cool, stir in roasted almonds and sherry. Whip cream until thick and then fold into mixture. Chill in a fridge until ready for use.

Press the pastry into four 7.5-cm (3-inch) tins, prick the bases with a fork and bake at 180°C/350°F/Gas Mark 4 for 20 minutes. Remove from the tins to cool.

Fill with the custard. Cut the figs into quarters and place 3 back to back on each tart centre to form a pyramid. Surround with slices of kiwi fruit and small scoops of papaya cut with a melon baller. Melt the apple jelly in a saucepan and brush on the fruit to glaze.

Paul Heathcote

Chocolate Orange Pots

SERVES 4

4 egg yolks

75g (3 oz) caster sugar

125ml (4 fl. oz) milk

175ml (6 fl. oz) cream

125g (4 oz) dark chocolate (or Terry's chocolate orange)

1 tsp orange arome (essence)

Cream egg yolks and sugar together. Boil milk and cream together and pour on to creamed yolks and sugar. Add chocolate and orange essence and allow to melt.

Pass through a fine sieve and pour into 4 heatproof pots. Allow to cool. Cook in bain-marie in a low oven at 170°C/325°F/Gas Mark 3 for approximately 30 minutes. Leave to cool and refrigerate before serving.

Steven Saunders

White Chocolate Mousse With Strawberries

SERVES 4

160g (5¹/₂ oz) good white chocolate

2 leaves gelatine

150ml (¹/₄ pint) double cream, very lightly whipped

225g (8 oz) strawberries, thinly sliced

100ml (3¹/₂ fl. oz) Kirsh (approximately)

pinch of icing sugar

Break chocolate into pieces and melt over a bain marie. Soak the gelatine in 1 tbsp warm water until dissolved. Mix this thoroughly into the melted chocolate. Add the semi-whipped double cream and stir in well. Pour into a terrine mould lined with cling film and allow to set in the fridge for 2–3 hours.

Marinate the strawberries in the Kirsch with the icing sugar. Serve a slice of the chocolate mousse on a bed of the strawberries.

Steven Saunders

Chocolate Marquise With Blackcurrant Coulis

SERVES 4-6

300g (10 oz) dark chocolate

175g (6 oz) honey

100g (3¹/₂ oz) unsalted butter

250ml (9 fl. oz) double cream

4 eggs, separated

1 small liqueur glass of Grande Marnier

icing sugar, to dust

Coulis
100ml (3¹/₂ fl. oz) water

50g (2 oz) caster sugar

200g (7 oz) frozen or fresh blackcurrants

¹/₂ lemon

Melt the chocolate and honey together over a bowl of hot water. Cream the butter and partially whip the cream. Add the cream and butter to the chocolate mixture. Add the yolks and liqueur and mix well.

Whisk the whites until soft peaks and fold into the chocolate mixture. Line a terrine mould with cling film and pour in marquise mixture. Chill until set, usually 4 hours or leave overnight. Turn out onto a chilled plate and cut into slices.

Bring water and sugar to the boil to form a syrup (5 to 7 minutes).

Reserve a few blackcurrants for decoration. Put remaining blackcurrants into food processor and add the juice of ¹/₂ lemon and the syrup. Blend together and pass through a sieve. Serve around the marquise garnished with some whole blackcurrants. Dust with icing sugar.

Microwave Chocolate Sponge With Tia Maria Syrup

SERVES 4

100g (3¹/₂ oz) unsalted butter

110g (3³/₄ oz) caster sugar

2 eggs

100g (3¹/₂ oz) plain flour

55g (2 oz) cocoa powder

1 tsp baking powder

Sauce

85g caster sugar

3 tbsp Tia Maria

white chocolate ice cream, to serve (optional)

Cream the butter and sugar and beat in the eggs. Add the sifted flour, cocoa powder and baking powder and mix in. Pour into 4 buttered dishes to just over half way.

Microwave each one on full power for 1 minute. Check and allow it to rest for a few seconds. The pudding should slide out of the mould easily, if it doesn't put it back into the microwave for another 30 seconds and repeat process.

Bring the water and sugar to the boil and just as you see a little colour, remove from heat and stir with a wooden spoon. Pour in the Tia Maria and stir in well. Serve over the chocolate sponge and finish with a scoop of white chocolate ice-cream (optional).

Greg Robinson

Tuscan Pudding Served With Strawberries And Warm Cointreau Flavoured Syrup

SERVES 4

vanilla sugar to sprinkle

375g (13 oz) sieved ricotta cheese

65g (2¹/₂ oz) ground almonds

45g (1¹/₂ oz) candied mixed peel

125g (4 oz) caster sugar

65g (2¹/₂ oz) sultanas

4 egg yolks

grated rind of a lemon

strawberries and whipped cream, to serve

Sugar Syrup

125g (4 oz) granulated sugar

225ml (8 fl. oz) water

Cointreau, to taste

Lightly butter a small savarin mould and sprinkle it with vanilla sugar. Mix together the ingredients for the pudding i.e. cheese, almonds, mixed peel, sugar, sultanas, egg yolks and lemon rind, and turn into the prepared mould.

Bake at approximately 170°C/325°F/Gas Mark 3 for 30 minutes or until firm to the touch.

Cool slightly and then turn out.

To make the syrup, dissolve the sugar in the water over a gentle heat. When completely dissolved boil the syrup for 3–4 minutes. Remove from the heat and add Cointreau to taste.

Spoon some of the syrup over the warm pudding. Fill the centre with strawberries and spoon over a little more of the syrup. Serve with extra whipped cream and the remaining syrup.

Greg Robinson

Baked Peaches with Marzipan on Toasted Brioche

SERVES 4

125g (4 oz) unsalted butter (softened)

4 slices day old brioche, 1.5cm (^{1}/$_2$ inch) thick

4 large ripe peaches

100g (3^1/$_2$ oz) caster sugar

125g (4 oz) marzipan

100g (3^1/$_2$ oz) slivered almonds

3 tbsp Amaretto (optional)

Greek yoghurt, to serve

Use most of the butter to spread on both sides of the brioche. Put the bread on to a baking sheet.

Halve and stone the peaches and cut into quarters. Arrange 4 quarters on each slice of bread, cut side up. Dredge the peaches with half the sugar. Chop the marzipan and sprinkle with the almonds equally over each piece of bread. Sprinkle the Amaretto over the peaches and dot with the remaining butter. Cover the 4 slices of brioche with a buttered piece of greaseproof paper.

Bake at 180°C/350°F/Gas Mark 4 for 30–40 minutes, uncovering and sprinkling with the remaining sugar halfway through cooking. The brioche should be crisp and golden and the marzipan browned. Serve warm with Greek yoghurt.

Greg Robinson

Walnut Pudding, Mixed Fruit And Rum Flavoured Cream

SERVES 4

8 walnuts

¹/₂ tsp ground cinnamon

5 eggs, separated

200g (7 oz) icing sugar

250ml (9 fl. oz) double cream

3 tbsp dark rum

selection of mixed fruit

Finely grate the walnuts in a food processor or coffee mill. Mix the walnuts with the ground cinnamon.

Beat the egg yolks and icing sugar until thick and creamy. Stir in the walnut mixture. Beat the egg white until stiff and fold into the walnut mixture.

Grease a heatproof mixing bowl with butter and sprinkle with granulated sugar. Pour in the batter. Tie foil over the pudding and cook for 45 minutes in a pan of lightly boiling water. The pudding should rise well.

Let the pudding cool and then turn out onto a serving plate. Whip the double cream until quite firm and then fold in the dark rum. To serve, put a slice of the pudding on a plate with a mixture of summer fruits and serve with the rum cream.

Little Apple and Strawberry Pies Made With An Orange Pastry

SERVES 4

Orange Shortcrust Pastry

225g (8 oz) plain flour

55g (2 oz) icing sugar

a pinch of salt

zest from 1 orange

225g (8 oz) unsalted butter

1 egg

1 tbsp milk

egg, to glaze

Filling

350g (12 oz) apples, peeled and cored

25g (1 oz) caster sugar

25g (1 oz) butter

juice of 1 orange

350g (12 oz) strawberries, roughly chopped

In a large bowl, sift the flour, icing sugar and salt together, stir in the orange zest. Rub in the butter to give a breadcrumb texture. Make a well in the flour, mix the egg with the milk and then gradually add to the flour to form a dough. Wrap in cling film and leave to rest in the refrigerator for at least 30 minutes.

Preheat the oven to 180°C/350°F/Gas Mark 4 and grease a tray of standard muffin tins. Make the filling, put the apples, sugar, butter and orange juice in a pan and simmer gently until the apples are just tender. Remove from the heat and allow to cool before adding the strawberry pieces.

Divide the pastry in half and roll out to 5mm (^{1}/4 inch) thick. Using a pastry cutter, cut out 10-cm (4-inch) circles and use to line the greased muffin tins, prick the base with a fork and leave to rest in the fridge for at least 15 minutes. Roll out the remaining pastry and using a 6-cm (2^1/2-)inch pastry cutter, cut out ten lids.

Line the pastry cases with greaseproof paper and baking beans and bake blind in the preheated oven for 5 minutes, remove the greaseproof paper and beans and continue to cook for 5 minutes. Spoon the apple and strawberry mixture into the pastry cases and then moisten the edges of the pastry with a little of the orange juice, place the lids on top and make a small hole in the top of each. Brush the tops with a little egg and bake for 20 minutes.

Serve the little pies with fresh custard.

Amanda Grant

Banana Tarts With Toffee Ice Cream

SERVES 8

Custard
850ml (1¹/₂ pints)
  milk

1 vanilla pod

8 egg yolks

100g (3¹/₂ oz) caster
  sugar

Ice cream
225g (8 oz) toffee

125ml (4 fl. oz)
  double cream

Tarts
250g (9 oz) frozen
  puff pastry,
  defrosted

4 large bananas,
  peeled and sliced
  diagonally

melted butter

icing sugar

Put the milk and vanilla pod in a saucepan and warm gently. In a large bowl, whisk the egg yolks and caster sugar until thick and creamy. Whisk the warm milk into the egg mixture, return to the heat, stir continuously without boiling, until the mixture coats the back of the spoon. Strain the custard and cool.

Place the toffee in a bag and using a rolling pin, crush into small pieces. Transfer 6 tablespoons of the custard to a small dish and put to one side. Pour the remaining custard into a freezerproof container and partly freeze for 5 hours. Whisk the double cream until soft, then fold into the frozen custard with the toffee pieces. Return to the freezer overnight.

Roll out the pastry to 5mm (¹/₄ inch) thick and cut 8 small circles, approximately 10 cm (4 inches) in diameter, generously prick the surface of each disc, then place on a lightly greased baking sheet. Leave in the refrigerator for at least half an hour. Preheat the oven to 220°C/425°F/Gas Mark 7.

Divide the reserved custard among the 8 pastry circles and then arrange the banana slices in a circle, leaving a tiny gap around the edge. Brush each tart with a little butter and dredge with icing sugar. Place in the preheated oven and cook for 15 minutes, or until thoroughly browned.

To serve, place the tarts on serving plates and arrange scoops of ice cream by the side. Dust with icing sugar.

Walnut And Pear Marmalade With Roquefort Sables

SERVES 6

Marmalade
100g (3¹/₂ oz)
  unsalted butter

1 lemon

100g (3¹/₂ oz) soft
  brown sugar

1.1kg (2¹/₂ lb) pears,
  peeled, cored and
  roughly chopped

2 cloves

2 tbsp brandy

175g (3¹/₄ oz) walnut
  pieces, toasted

Roquefort
Sables
100g (3¹/₂ oz) plain
  flour

100g (3¹/₂ oz) butter

100g (3¹/₂ oz)
  Roquefort cheese,
  broken into pieces

freshly ground black
  pepper

1 egg, beaten, to
  glaze

Roquefort cheese, to
  serve

Put the butter, lemon juice and zest in a small saucepan and warm gently, until the butter is melted. Stir in the sugar, add the pears and cloves. Cover, cook until the pears are soft – approximately 10 minutes.

Meanwhile, make the sables. Preheat the oven to 190°C/375°F/Gas Mark 5. Sieve the flour into a large bowl, rub in the butter until the mixture resembles fine breadcrumbs. Add the roquefort and season with freshly ground black pepper, mix together to form a dough.

Roll out the dough about 5mm (¹/₄ inch) thick on a floured surface, and cut into about 20 triangles, rounds and squares. Put on a greased baking sheet, brush with a little beaten egg and bake in the preheated oven for about 10–15 minutes or until golden.

When the pears are soft, remove the lid and reduce the excess liquid, this will take approximately 20 minutes. Add the brandy and cook for 1 minute. Cool, then add the walnuts. Be careful not to caramelise the pears. Leave the sables to cool for 5 minutes before transferring them to a wire cooling rack (to prevent them from crumbling). Serve the sables with the marmalade and a little roquefort cheese.

Amanda Grant

Apple Charlotte With Toffee Sauce

SERVES 4

1 lemon

1.5kg (3lb) apples, peeled, cored and thinly sliced

150ml (¹/₄ pint) apple juice

150ml (¹/₄ pint) water

150g (5 oz) soft brown sugar

1 tsp ground cinnamon

¹/₂ tsp freshly grated nutmeg

175g (6 oz) sponge fingers (approximately 20)

Toffee Sauce

150ml (¹/₄ pint) double cream

100g (3¹/₂ oz) butter

100g (3¹/₂ oz) soft brown sugar

Peel off 2 strips of zest from the lemon and put in a large bowl. Squeeze the lemon's juice and add to the bowl. Add the apple slices to the lemon juice and zest, cover and leave to macerate for at least 1 hour. Pour the apple juice and water into a large frying pan, add the sugar and spices, place over a gentle heat until the sugar has dissolved, stirring constantly.

Simmer for 5 minutes and then add the apples and their juices, turning a few times, for 2–3 minutes, or until the apples are tender. Take the apples and lemon zest out of the pan and reduce the juice to a syrup.

Line a 1-litre (2-pint) pudding basin with cling film. Soak the sponge fingers in the syrup until they are slightly soft and use to line the basin. Spoon the apples in the basin and cover with the remaining sponge fingers. Drizzle a little syrup over the top and place a serving plate over the top, weight it down and leave for 30 minutes. Turn the pudding up the right way and peel off the cling film.

To make the toffee sauce, put all the ingredients in a saucepan and place over a gentle heat, stir continuously until the butter and sugar has melted. Bring the sauce to the boil fast for 5 minutes, serve warm with the Apple Charlotte.

Banana, Kiwi And Lychee Spring Rolls

SERVES 4

2 mangoes, peeled and stoned

3 firm bananas

2 kiwi fruit, peeled and sliced

6 lychees, stoned and sliced

9 spring roll wrappers

1 lemon

3 tsp soft light brown sugar

1 egg white, beaten

oil, for frying

icing sugar, to dust

lychees, to decorate

Place the mango flesh in a liquidiser, purée until smooth. Cover and refrigerate.

Cut the banana in half lengthways, place cut side up and arrange 3/4 kiwi slices on top, without overlapping them. Repeat with the lychee slices. Place the other banana half on top and then cut into three crosswise. Repeat with the remaining bananas, kiwi and lychees.

Place a spring roll wrapper on the work surface with a corner facing you. Place a stuffed banana horizontally across the middle of the wrapper. Sprinkle a little lemon zest and brown sugar over the fruit, then fold the bottom corner of the wrapper over the banana and tuck it under. Fold in the sides and roll the banana almost up to the end. Brush the top corner with a little egg white, roll up and press firmly to seal. Repeat with the other bananas.

Preheat 5-cm (2-inches) of oil in a large frying pan or wok and fry the rolls, 3 at a time, until golden brown, about 4 minutes, turning occasionally. Remove with a slotted spoon and drain on kitchen paper. Repeat with the rest of the rolls. Dust with the icing sugar and serve immediately with a little of the fresh mango sauce, decorate with lychees.

Amanda Grant

Peach Pastry With A Raspberry And Cinnamon Sauce

SERVES 4

250g (9 oz) ready-rolled puff pastry, defrosted

1 egg, beaten

12 ripe peaches, stoned and halved

6 tsp water

75g (3 oz) soft brown sugar

1 tbsp dessert wine

icing sugar, to dust

Sauce

700g (1½ lb) raspberries

50g (2 oz) caster sugar

2 tsp ground cinnamon

1 cinnamon stick

Preheat the oven to 200°C/400°F/Gas Mark 6. Roll out the pastry to 33 x 23cm (13 x 9 inch) rectangle and trim off 2.5-cm (1-inch) strips from all sides, then brush the edges with a beaten egg. Transfer to a greased baking sheet and place the pastry strips on top of the pastry around the edge, to form a case, trimming to fit. Knock up the edges and decorate by scoring pretty lines, brush the edges with egg again and leave to rest for at least 30 minutes. Arrange the peach halves in the small rectangle, spoon the wine over the peaches and sprinkle with sugar. Place in the preheated oven and bake for 20–25 minutes or until the pastry is golden and crisp and the peaches have started to caramelise.

To make the sauce, put the raspberries, sugar, ground cinnamon and cinnamon stick in a saucepan and heat gently until the sugar dissolves and the raspberries begin to fall apart. Remove from the heat and take out the cinnamon stick, transfer to a liquidiser and purée until smooth. Sieve, spoon into a serving bowl and chill until required.

To serve, dust the tart with icing sugar and place (preferably on the garden table in the sunshine) with the sauce next to it, allowing guests to cut a slice and drizzle with the raspberry and cinnamon sauce.

Amanda Grant

Little Tulips Of A Chilled Aromatic Plum And Rosemary Yoghurt Ice

SERVES 4

4 sheets filo pastry

25g (1 oz) butter, melted

350g (12 oz) ripe dark skinned plums, stoned and quartered

150ml (¼ pint) red wine

150ml (¼ pint) water

75g (3 oz) caster sugar

4 rosemary sprigs

1 piece orange (zest)

250g (9 oz) mascarpone

175ml (6 fl. oz) Greek yoghurt

50g (2 oz) Amaretti biscuits, crumbled

Preheat the oven to 180°C/350°F/Gas Mark 4. Brush the outside of four little pudding tins or small ramekins with half of the melted butter and place upside down on a baking sheet, cut each sheet of filo pastry into two 15-cm (6-inch) squares. Brush each pastry sheet with the remaining butter. Place a square of pastry over the prepared tin. Place another square at a right angle to the first. Repeat with the remaining tins. (It is important at this stage to make the top of the pastry as flat as possible as this will become the bottom).

Put the pastry into the preheated oven and bake for 15 minutes, cool slightly. Take the pastry cases off the tins or ramekins and place on a baking sheet. Return to the oven for 5 minutes. Place on a cooling rack and leave to cool.

Put the plums, red wine, water and sugar in a saucepan with the rosemary and orange zest. Bring to the boil then simmer for 3 minutes, long enough to soften the plums without losing their shape.

Drain the plums (discard the rosemary and orange zest) and put half of them into a food processor (reserve the rest), for one minute or until thick and chunky. Return the juice to the saucepan. Boil for 5–8 minutes until syrupy. Reduce to 150ml (¼ pint). Allow to cool, strain, chill and put to one side.

Mix together the mascarpone and Greek yoghurt and fold in the chopped processed plums. Pour the mixture into a shallow container, cover the surface with clingfilm. Chill for at least 2 hours.

To serve, scoop the yoghurt plum mixture into the pastry cases, drizzle with the syrup and top with reserved plums and crushed Amaretti biscuits.

Aaron Patterson

Apricot Tatin

SERVES 4
200g (7 oz) caster sugar
125g (4 oz) butter
100g (3½ oz) puff pastry
8 apricots
a dash of Amaretto

Brush a medium-sized ovenproof frying pan with melted butter and leave to set. Then dust with sugar.

Put the remaining sugar and butter in a pan and whisk over a medium heat until they form a golden brown caramel. Pour this into the sugared pan.

Slice the apricots in half and remove the stone. Place the halves in the pan upside down and splash with a little Amaretto.

Roll out the puff pastry very thinly and cut into a square a little larger than the top of the frying pan. Place this on top of the apricots and tuck it around and under them.

Bake in the oven for about 20–25 minutes at 220°C/425°F/Gas Mark 7. When the tatin is baked, turn out straight away on to the serving plate.

Summer Pudding

SERVES 8

1 stoneground
    wholemeal loaf of
    bread

175g (6 oz)
    blackcurrants

175g (6 oz)
    redcurrants

175g (6 oz)
    raspberries

175g (6 oz) cherries

175g (6 oz)
    blueberries or
    bilberries

175g (6 oz) small
    strawberries

4–6 tbsp caster sugar
    (dependent on the
    acidity of the fruit)

1 lemon, made into
    twirls of zest

To Serve
icing sugar

mint leaves

pouring cream or
    crème fraîche (into
    which you have
    stirred a few vanilla
    seeds and a dusting
    of icing sugar)

Strip stalks and hulls from all the fruit. Stone cherries. Reserve a few attractive little bunches of each fruit to garnish the puddings. Put all fruit into a pan with the caster sugar and zest, and cook only until the juices flow. Check the sweetness and add more sugar if necessary. Pour fruit through a colander over a dish to catch the juices. Remove the zest.

Trim crusts off bread and slice it fairly thinly. Cut out 4 circles to fit the bottoms of 4 pudding tins. Cut out rectangular strips, the height of the pudding tins and about 3cm (1¹/₂ inch) wide. Soak it both sides in the deep red juices. Now line the tins with the soaked bread, making sure that there are no gaps. You will need to overlap the strips slightly. Pack fruit into pudding tins, right to the top. Cut out another 4 circles of bread to fit the tops. Dip these also in the syrup. Top the puddings.

Wrap the puddings enclosed in cling food wrap, twisting the excess underneath. Stand them on a tray. Put a second tray on top and weight them down. Chill in the refrigerator overnight.

Liquidise all remaining cooked fruit with the remaining fruit syrup and pass through a fine sieve into a clean container. You should now have a coating fruit sauce. Chill until the next day.

Trim off any excess bread on the base of the pudding. Run a small thin knife round the sides and, giving a good shake, turn the puddings out on to plates. Pour a little sauce over and round the puddings, making sure the top and sides are coated with it and have a deep gloss. Arrange the sprigs of berries on top and round the sides attractively, together with the mint leaves. Dust lightly with icing sugar. Serve with a jug of pouring cream or a spoonful of vanilla crème fraîche.

Amanda Grant

Hazelnut-Crust Tart With A Sour Cream And Blueberry Topping

SERVES 4

Crust
200g (7 oz) hazelnuts

6 tbsp light soft brown sugar

25g (1 oz) unsalted butter, melted

Filling
175ml (6 fl. oz) sour cream

175g (6 oz) white chocolate, broken into small pieces

Topping
450g (1lb) blueberries

3 tbsp crème de cassis

1 tbsp icing sugar, to dust

Preheat the oven to 170°C/325°F/Gas Mark 3. Finely chop the hazelnuts and sugar in a food processor. Add the butter and process until moist clumps form. Divide the dough among four 10-cm (4-inch) fluted loose-bottomed flan tins. Push the nut mixture evenly up the sides and across the bottom. Bake in the preheated oven for 45 minutes. Remove from the oven and cool.

Put the sour cream in a thick-based saucepan and warm through. Add the chocolate. Remove from the heat. Stir until melted and smooth. Pour into the hazelnut crusts and leave in the fridge until set.

Put the blueberries and crème de cassis into a small saucepan, bring up to a simmering point. Turn the heat off and leave for a few minutes.

Remove the tarts from their casts and place on individual plates. Spoon the blueberries over the top and dust with a little icing sugar.

Strawberry And Rose-Petal Shortcake

Serves 8

Shortcake
450g (1 lb) butter

225g (8 oz) caster sugar (infused with vanilla)

450g (2 oz) plain flour sieved

225g (8 oz) semolina

Filling
675g (1¹/₂ oz) ripe strawberries, reserve 9 perfect ones for garnish and slice the rest

300ml (¹/₂ pint) double cream

3 large red roses from old-fashioned scented roses (not sprayed with insecticide)

1 tbsp icing sugar

¹/₂ tsp rose water

2 tsp lemon juice

Decoration
2 rose buds

1 egg white, lightly beaten

caster sugar (in a fine dredger)

Cream butter and sugar until light and fluffy. Gradually work in the flour and semolina. You will have to use your hand to blend in the last bits into a dough. Knead lightly until smooth. Divide into 2 pieces and roll out each piece carefully on to a floured surface. This is a very fragile dough. Using a fluted pastry cutter, cut out 16 circles. Lift on to greased and floured baking sheets and put in refrigerator to rest and chill.

Prepare rose cream. Put the lemon juice into a basin. Remove perfect petals from the roses and crush scented rose petals in your hand and drop them into the lemon juice, turning them over gently to keep the colour fresh. Add cream, together with the icing sugar and rose water. Stir all together and leave to infuse for 30 minutes.

Bake the shortcakes at 170°C/325°F/Gas Mark 3 for about 25 minutes until tinged golden only. Remove to cooling trays with a palette knife. They will crisp as they cool.

Sieve the cream, discarding the petals. Whisk until it is firm. Spread each shortcake with cream, then sliced strawberries, then top with a second shortcake. Dredge with fine caster sugar. Brush the rose buds with beaten egg white and dredge with caster sugar. Allow to set and dry before using to decorate the plate of shortcakes.

Tessa Bramley

Raspberry Queen Of Puddings

SERVES 4

Custard

600ml (1 pint) double cream (reserve 1 tbsp for decoration)

1 vanilla pod

5 egg yolks

1 tsp cornflour

1 tbsp caster sugar

55g (2 oz) fresh white breadcrumbs

2 lemons, grated zest

450g (1lb) fresh raspberries

1 tbsp icing sugar

3 egg whites

pinch of salt

4 tbsp caster sugar

1 tbsp flaked almonds

Split the vanilla pod lengthways, scrape out seeds into the double cream in a saucepan. Add pod as well.

Whisk egg yolks, cornflour and sugar together in a bowl. (The tiny amount of cornflour in the custard does not thicken it. It is merely a trick to prevent the eggs from curdling.)

Bring vanilla cream to boiling point. Remove pod. Allow cream to rise in pan and then pour quickly on to egg mixture, whisking continuously until mixture thickens. Pass custard through a fine sieve.

Sprinkle breadcrumbs into 4 ovenproof dishes. Add lemon zest and mix in. Pour the hot custard into the dishes. Leave to chill for a couple of hours.

Purée 125g (4 oz) raspberries with the icing sugar and press through a sieve to make a coulis. Spread over 1 tbsp raspberry coulis on each dish and top with the raspberries, reserving 125g (4 oz) for decoration.

Make meringue. Whisk egg whites in a bowl with a pinch of salt, until they form stiff peaks. Whisk in 3 tbsp sugar and bring back to stiff, glossy peaks. Pile meringue on top of custard in rough peaks – do not attempt to spread meringue, but make certain custard is completely covered. Scatter remaining caster sugar and flaked almonds over meringue. Bake in preheated oven for 25–30 minutes, until top of meringue is crisp with lightly golden peaks.

Serve plated decorated with the reserved raspberries and remaining raspberry coulis. It looks very pretty with the reserved cream swirled through the coulis with the tip of a small knife.

Iced Strawberry Soufflé

SERVES 4

150ml (¹/₄ pint) egg
whites
(approximately 5–6
eggs)

250g (9 oz) sugar

400ml (14 fl. oz)
whipping cream

450g (1 lb) fresh
strawberries, plus a
few for decoration

1 tbsp icing sugar

mint sprigs, to
decorate

Line four individual soufflé pots with silicone paper and set aside. Put 300g (10 oz) of the strawberries in a food processor and blend to a purée. Put 50g (2 oz) strawberries in a pan with the icing sugar and heat gently until the juices run. Press through a sieve to make a coulis. Whip the cream to soft peaks.

Bring the sugar to the boil in a thick-bottomed pan until it reaches thread stage (102°C/215°F). Two cold spoons dipped in together and gently parted will make a short 'thread' between them.

Whisk the egg whites until stiff and pour the sugar on to the whites slowly while continuing to whisk. When cool, add the fruit purée and fold in the whipped cream. Pour the mixture into the soufflé pots and place in the freezer until completely set.

Mix the remaining strawberries and the coulis together. Scoop out the centre of the soufflé (saving what you have taken out) and fill the hollow with strawberry mix. With a hot palette knife, smooth back over the reserved part of the soufflé. Decorate with fresh strawberries and mint. Serve immediately.

Aaron Patterson

Vanilla-Flavoured Fromage Frais With A Compote Of Summer Berries

SERVES 4

300ml (¹/₂ pint) fromage frais

2 vanilla pods

200ml (7 fl. oz) double cream

icing sugar, to taste

400g (14 oz) selection of mixed summer berries

4 sprigs fresh mint

Place the fromage frais into a mixing bowl. Add the vanilla seeds. Lightly whip the double cream with icing sugar to taste and add to the fromage frais. Place into small dariole moulds (which have been lined with cling film) and refrigerate for 1 hour.

Purée 100g (3¹/₂ oz) of summer fruits with 20g (³/₄ oz) icing sugar, and pass through a fine sieve. Place the whole fruits into a bowl and add the purée. Turn out the fromage frais moulds into the centre of a plate. Place the berries around and decorate with mint.

Aaron Patterson

Gratin Of Summer Berries

SERVES 1 – 2

1 egg yolk

100g selection of berries

50g (2 oz) sugar

1 vanilla pod

3 tbsp cream

2 tbsp sweet wine

1 lemon (juice)

Whisk the egg yolk with the sugar in a bowl over boiling water until it doubles in volume and is thick and creamy. Whisk in the vanilla essence, cream, wine and lemon juice. Fold in the berries. Spoon into a flameproof dish and glaze under a hot grill.

Serve with sorbet, ice cream or crème fraîche.

Jean Davies

Baked Bananas In Lemon And Rum Sauce

SERVES 4

4 bananas (large, firm but ripe)

Sauce

1 tbsp grated lemon rind

2 tbsp lemon juice

2 tbsp demerara sugar

3 tbsp orange marmalade

2–3 tbsp water

2 tbsp dark rum

fresh mint leaves and julienne strips of orange rind, to decorate

fresh cream, to serve

Preheat oven to 200°C/400°F/Gas Mark 6. Trim ends of the bananas, removing about 1 cm (1/2 inch) from each end, cut a slit through the skin that extends the length of the fruit. Arrange them on a baking sheet and bake for 15 minutes or until the skins turn black.

Meanwhile, mix together the lemon rind and the juice, sugar, marmalade and water in a pan. Bring to the boil for 1 minute, then transfer to a serving dish.

Add the rum to the sauce in the serving dish and stir in. As soon as the bananas are cool, remove the skins and place them in the sauce. Coat the bananas on all sides with the sauce. Slice the bananas into diagonal chunks, decorate with mint leaves and orange rind. Serve at room temperature with cream

Steven Saunders

Banana Pancakes With Toffee Sauce

SERVES 4

3 bananas, sliced

2 oranges

75g (3 oz) caster sugar

Pancakes
2 eggs

2 tsp caster sugar

250ml (9 fl. oz) milk

125g (4 oz) plain flour

Butterscotch Sauce
150g (5 oz) butter

250g (9 oz) soft brown sugar

125ml (4 fl. oz) double cream

To prepare pancakes, whisk eggs and sugar together. Add sifted flour and blend in with a wooden spoon. Pass through a sieve into a clean bowl. Heat a little oil in a fying pan. When smoking, tip off the oil. Make the pancakes in the usual way. You will need 1 per person. Extra pancakes can be packed between sheets of greaseproof paper in a plastic bag and frozen for later use.

Prepare the sauce by melting the butter and sugar until it caramelises and add the double cream. Stir in and, if necessary, pass through a sieve.

Line a dariole or a ramekin mould with a pancake and warm the slices of banana in the butterscotch sauce. Fill each pancake mould, fold the pancake over the top and turn out on to a plate. Serve with a little more sauce and garnish with a confit of orange zest.

To make the confit of orange zest. Remove the zest from the oranges in long strips with a zester. Blanch the zest twice and refresh. Stir the orange zest with the 75g (3 oz) of sugar over a medium heat until it crisps and caramelises.

Pear Tart Tatin

SERVES 4

5 large pears

100g (3¹/₂ oz)
  unsalted butter

100g (3¹/₂ oz) caster
  sugar

225g (8 oz) puff
  pastry

beaten egg, to glaze

225g (8 oz) clotted
  cream, to serve

Poaching
Syrup

250ml (9 fl. oz) water

175g (6 oz) caster
  sugar

1 stick cinnamon

splash of white wine

In a large saucepan put all the poaching syrup ingredients and bring to the boil. Peel pears and drop into the syrup and cook until tender (approximately 10 minutes). Remove immediately. Core the pears and slice in half.

In a large ovenproof frying pan melt the butter and add the caster sugar. Cook gently until a golden caramel and add the halves of pears with the rounded side into the pan.

Roll out the pastry thinly and prick with a fork. Cut it to 1.5cm (¹/₂ inch) larger than the pan it is fitting into. Press pastry into shape over the top of the pan and pears and brush with egg wash.

Bake at 200°C/400°F/Gas Mark 6 for 20 minutes or until golden brown on the top. Turn out on to a plate and serve the clotted cream on the side or over the top.

Mark Wogan

Pineapple Croustade

SERVES 4

100g (3¹/₂ oz)
   unsalted butter

1 large pineapple,
   cored, skinned and
   chopped

3 tbsp brandy

175g (6 oz) caster
   sugar

250g (9 oz) filo
   pastry

Rum Cream

200ml (7 fl. oz)
   whipping cream

2 tbsp icing sugar

5 tbsp rum

Melt 60g (2¹/₂ oz) butter in a frying pan, add the pineapple, brandy and half the sugar. Cook until tender about 5 to 6 minutes.

Preheat the oven to 200°C/400°C/Gas Mark 6. Melt the remaining butter and spread a little over the base of a 23-cm (9-inch) loose-bottomed flan ring.

Lay one sheet of filo in the ring. Then brush with butter, repeat this twice. Spoon the pineapple on to the base and fold in the corners. Butter the remaining sheets. Gently scrunch them and place on top.

Sprinkle the remaining sugar over the top and bake for 20 minutes, then reduce the temperature to 180°C/350°F/Gas Mark 4 and bake for 20 minutes. Whip the cream until it starts to hold its shape, then add the icing sugar and rum. Remove the croustade from the oven. Cut into wedges and serve with the Rum-Flavoured Cream.

Orange And Raspberry Terrine

SERVES 4

600ml (1 pint) orange juice

15g (¹/₂ oz) powdered gelatine

50g (2 oz) caster sugar

3 oranges, segmented

250g (9 oz) raspberries

Sauce

250g (9 oz) strawberries

50g (2 oz) caster sugar

2 tsp balsamic vinegar

1 tsp fresh ground black pepper

Pour 100ml (3¹/₂ fl. oz) of juice into a pan warm it gently and dissolve the gelatine, then add the remaining liquid and remove from the heat. Add the sugar then pour half the juice into a 1.3 litre (2¹/₄ pint) tin lined with cling film. Chill this until it has almost set, then scatter a selection of the fruits over the jelly. Add the remainder of the juice very gently and chill until almost completely set. Add remaining fruit and chill again until completely set.

To make the sauce, place all the ingredients in a blender and process until smooth. To serve, turn out the terrine. Remove cling film and slice with a sharp knife that has been dipped in hot water. Place two thin slices on to plate and drizzle over the sauce.

Oranges In Zabaglione

SERVES 4

4 egg yolks

100g (3¹/₂ oz) caster sugar

175ml (6 fl. oz) Marsala wine

4 oranges, segmented

Beat the yolks with the sugar until creamy and dissolved. Add the wine and beat a little longer. Place the bowl over a pan of boiling water and whisk until thick and foamy.

Preheat the grill to its highest setting. Arrange the oranges in individual heatproof dishes. Pour equal amounts of the zabaglione over each one. Brown under the grill and serve.

Mark Wogan

Highland Berry Brûlée

SERVES 4

300ml (¹/₂ pint)
double cream

1 vanilla pod

2 egg yolks

4 tbsp caster sugar

200g (7 oz) mixture
of loganberries and
tayberries

5 tbsp Scotch whisky

Bring the cream and vanilla pod to the boil, then beat the eggs and half the sugar until creamy and add to the cream mix and remove the pod.
Simmer until the mix coats the back of the spoon.

Cook the fruit in the Scotch until soft (about 15 minutes on a low heat). Divide the fruit evenly among four small soufflé dishes and pour over the custard.

Preheat the oven to 170°C/325°F/Gas Mark 3 and place the dishes in a bain marie in the oven for 12 minutes. Remove from the oven and for best results, refrigerate overnight. Heat the grill to its highest setting. Sprinkle the custards with the remaining caster sugar and place under the grill until it blackens. Leave to cool and serve.

Jean Davies

Pinenut Izarra Torte

SERVES 4

1 small orange

1 small lemon

2 tbsp Izarra (a liqueur from the Basque region of Spain)

4 tbsp olive oil

55g (2 oz) pinenuts

3 free-range eggs

100g (3¹/₂ oz) caster sugar

100g (3¹/₂ oz) plain flour

1 tbsp icing sugar

double cream, to serve (optional)

olive oil and plain flour, for dusting

fresh mint leaves, to decorate

Lemon Sauce

2 tbsp lemon curd

1-2 tbsp lemon juice

4 tbsp double cream

Brush a 20-cm (8-inch) spring-release or a loose-based cake tin with oil, then dust with flour, shaking off any excess. Grate the zest from the orange and lemon. Mix together the Izarra and olive oil. Roughly chop the pinenuts.

Set an electric whisk to its fastest speed and whisk together the eggs and the sugar for about 6 minutes or until pale and thick. Set the whisk to its lowest speed. Add the orange and lemon zest and the sieved flour and whisk until just combined. Using a spatula or large metal spoon gently fold in the Izarra and the oil.

Pour into a prepared tin, bake at 150°C/300°F/Gas Mark 2 for 20 minutes. Remove from the oven and quickly sprinkle with pinenuts, pushing them gently into the top. Dust with the icing sugar and return to the oven for another 10 minutes or until a skewer inserted into the centre of the cake comes out clean.

Allow the torte to cool for 10 minutes and then flash under a hot grill for 1 minute or until the sugar begins to caramelise and the nuts turn golden brown. Remove the base and serve warm or cold with cream and lemon sauce. Decorate with fresh mint leaves.

To make the Lemon Sauce, place all the ingredients in a heavy-bottomed pan , then heat gently stirring all the time until smooth and well blended.

Paul Heathcote

Sweet Bourekia With Manouri

SERVES 4

4 sheets filo pastry

300g (10 oz) Manouri or other soft cheese

50g (2 oz) icing sugar

50g (2 oz) cinnamon

4 tsp honey

50g (2 oz) toasted almond flakes

vegetable oil, for brushing

Place two sheets of filo pastry together by brushing one sheet with vegetable oil and laying the second on top. Cut out six circles and brush oil on to one side.

Place 25g (a little less than 1 oz) of cheese inside each circle and fold over to make a pastie. Repeat with other two sheets of filo and remaining cheese. Deep fry in hot oil until light brown. Place in the centre of a plate, sprinkle almonds on top, dust with sugar and cinnamon mix and spoon the honey over.

Brandy Snap Baskets

SERVES 4

125g (4 oz) unsalted butter

125g (4 oz) unrefined soft brown sugar

4 tbsp golden syrup

125g (4 oz) plain flour

1 tsp ground ginger

Make the mixture the day before you need it. The snaps are thinner and crisper if the mixture is at least a day old.

Heat butter, sugar and syrup in a pan over a low heat until melted. Sieve together the flour and ginger. Remove pan from heat and sieve in the flour slowly mixing as you go. Beat until smooth. Pour into clean container. Chill in refrigerator until ready to use.

Preheat oven to 170°C/325°F/Gas Mark 3. Turn several baking sheets upside down and lightly grease the undersides. It is much easier to remove the brandy snaps from a tray with no side lips.

Place walnut-sized pieces on to the trays and spread out into circles with your fingertips. Don't attempt more than 2 per tray. Bake in a preheated oven for 5–7 minutes until golden and set. Remove from oven and leave to settle for a minute or so. The snaps will have a lacy surface.

Lift biscuits from tin using a palette knife and drape immediately over a ramekin or pudding basin (or cut the base of a lemon and use that) squeezing into a tulip shape whilst still warm. Repeat until you have used up the mixture. Store in an airtight tin until needed.

Fill with a selection of ice creams, fruits, or sorbets to make a wonderfully light summer dessert.

Index